W9-BQK-684

WITH THE COMPLIMENTS

OF THE ~~AUTHOR~~ Editors

The McGinleys

(Sister Myron, Wm., Sylvester, and Mary E.)

AND

THE BRUCE PUBLISHING COMPANY

NEW YORK MILWAUKEE CHICAGO

Mrs. J. A. Fell 10 De Sabla Rd., San Mateo, Calif.

A TRAPPIST
WRITES HOME

A TRAPPIST WRITES HOME

LETTERS OF

Abbot Gerard McGinley, o.c.s.o.

TO HIS FAMILY

+

Copy 1

INTRODUCTION BY

FATHER RAYMOND, O.C.S.O.

THE BRUCE PUBLISHING COMPANY

MILWAUKEE

IMPRIMI POTEST:

REV. FATHER M. PAUL BOURNE, O.C.S.O.
Abbey of Our Lady of the Holy Ghost
Conyers, Georgia

NIHIL OBSTAT:

JOHN A. SCHULIEN, S.T.D.
Censor librorum

IMPRIMATUR:

✠ WILLIAM E. COUSINS
Archbishop of Milwaukee
February 3, 1960

Library of Congress Catalog Card Number: 60-10195

TO THE KING AND QUEEN
OF HEAVEN AND EARTH
AND TO PRINCESS THÉRÈSE OF LISIEUX

PREFACE

A SINGLE letter written by a person may reveal more of his real character than a few volumes written about him. This simple idea served as a starter for this collection of letters written by the teen-ager Bernard McGinley, who became Father Gerard and eventually Abbot Gerard, of the Trappist-Cistercian monastery at Piffard, New York. The letters prove that St. Thérèse's "Little Way" is for souls who desire to be strong and virile lovers of God and man.

The compilers are grateful to the following for their permission and encouragement in working out this project: The Most Reverend James E. Kearney, Bishop of Rochester, New York; the Most Reverend Dom M. Gabriel Sortais, Abbot General of the Trappist Cistercians; the Right Reverend Dom M. James Fox, Abbot of Our Lady of Gethsemani, and community, Trappist, Kentucky; the Right Reverend Walter Helmstetter, Abbot of Our Lady of the Genesee, and community, Piffard, New York; and to the Reverend Mother Richarda Peters, O.S.B., and community, St. Benedict's Priory, St. Joseph, Minnesota.

THE MCGINLEYS

CONTENTS

A TRAPPIST WRITES HOME

INTRODUCTION

DOM GERARD MCGINLEY is the man who quietly shatters accepted definitions of some of our most sacred things — only to reveal to us the essences of the things defined. Meet, in his letters, a monk who uses many of our most familiar concepts, only to make them look so strange that we actually see them for the first time. Let this Trappist Cistercian, as novice, professed monk, and abbot, take you into the intimacy of his cloistered life that he may show you some of the deepest mysteries of God — and prove how personal they are to you.

The Trappist life is not something; it is *Someone*. Hence these letters will not only let you in to what is actually a very secluded section of God's Workshop, but grant you an unobstructed view of Omnipotence at one of His mightiest works. For, as you follow him as a teen-ager from his home in Minnesota to New Jersey, then to Gethsemani, Kentucky, where, for almost a quarter of a century, you will watch him in the Trappist routine, it will gradually come home to you that what you are actually doing is watching God as He goes about a task much more mysterious — and of far greater magnificence — than the one He accomplished when He called to Nothingness and evoked the Universe. For what He effected in the soul of this young monk was something infinitely more enduring than what He achieved when first He created the sun, stars, and moon. It was a task almost infinitely more delicate — and difficult; for Nothingness had to answer His summons, whereas the John Bernard McGinley who was to become, first, Frater Gerard, then Father Gerard, and finally Dom Gerard McGinley, could have said "no" to God at any time.

Dom Gerard McGinley provides the solution to all that puzzlement in a series of letters, never written for publication, but which serve as revelation not only of the secret of his life, but the secret of all right living. That is a secret Trappist silence keeps reminding the world of: that the most realistic definition ever given of man is one who is *capax Dei*, "capable of being filled with God." Dom Gerard McGinley lived that definition to the letter.

That is a sample of what is meant when it is said that he shatters definitions only to reveal the essence of the things defined. How much more inspiring and ultimately how much more exact it is to realize that men are "persons capable of being filled with God," than it is to recognize them simply as "rational animals." But what he did to our commonly accepted notion of a person he does even more devastatingly, and with the same exhilarating effect, to our current idea of personality.

Few people ever left the presence of Gerard McGinley, whether it was while he was a simple monk, guest master, retreat master, the prior of Gethsemani, or abbot of Genesee, without wondering just what it was about the man that had affected them. They knew they had felt a rare human warmth in his presence, but were at a loss to account for it. For while the man was ever gracious and affable, there was nothing about him of that glamor we usually associate with personalities that set people aglow. Moreover, one carried from his presence a surprisingly satisfying sense of peace and a calm inner joy. Yet he was not endowed with any of those abilities all expect to find in one who is named, rightly or wrongly, "a powerful personality."

These letters reveal how from his earliest years as monk to his unexpected and, if the term is ever allowable, his untimely death in Dijon, France, this man had labored incessantly to fill himself with God. The result was felt by merely coming into his presence. And once again he makes us readjust our ideas: the truly powerful human personality is that one which radiates Divinity.

What he does to our usual ideas of person and personality, he does even more completely and convincingly to our commonly accepted notions of liberty, maturity, and integrity.

In a letter written on the train taking him south, he tells his sister that she could regard her little brother as "a prisoner" and that it was his intention to be a prisoner for life. Now it is at least a bit unusual for anyone to go looking for liberty by becoming a prisoner; even if one intends to become what young McGinley called himself: "a prisoner of love." Yet the faultless insight of this teen-ager is comparable in every way with that of

George Bernard Shaw, who one day wrote to Dame Laurentia, Abbess of the Benedictine Monastery of Stanbrook: "When we are next touring in your neighborhood I shall again shake your bars and look longingly at the freedom on the other side of them."

What Dame Laurentia and Dom Gerard enjoyed behind their cloistering bars was that liberty proclaimed by St. Paul to his Romans, Corinthians, and Galatians; the liberty John the Evangelist presented as possible for every man who breathes: the liberty that comes from the Son of God. "If therefore, the Son makes you free, you will be free indeed" (Jn. 8:36). These two cloistered religious knew that "freedom wherewith Christ has made us free" (Gal. 4:31).

As John Bernard McGinley rode down through Pennsylvania that cold day in late January of 1926 he may not have known with fullest clarity that, like St. Paul's Galatians, he had been "called unto liberty" (Gal. 5:13), but the fruit of such a calling and of such a liberty was already in his heart. As the years mounted and he cloistered himself the more closely with God, this happiness grew, for his inner freedom became ever greater. St. Paul accounted for it all when he wrote: "Where the Spirit of God is, there is freedom" (2 Cor. 3:17).

We who have waged a World War for what we called "four freedoms" can learn much about liberty from this man who surrendered himself unconditionally to God. From him we can also learn much about maturity. Dom Gerard in his letters tells us that growing up rightly actually consists in growing down, and that if we would manifest genuine maturity before men, we must first show ourselves little children before God.

Here his hand is firmly on essences; for his doctrine is based on that relation of ours to God which is not only a real relation, but one that is intrinsically constitutive; for it is a relation that not only tells how we came into being, but also accounts for our continuing to be; it is a relation so durable as to be destructible only by an act of annihilation on the part of God. This young man as a very young monk came to realize that we swaggeringly independent humans are as utterly dependent on God for our next breath and heartbeat as we were for our first. Gradually Gerard McGinley came to know the whole vast universe of connotations contained in that right, privilege, and duty which is ours to call God "Father." That is rare maturity. For it gives one a poise nothing can disturb. That was the imperturbability which marked Dom Gerard McGinley — and that was its source.

But make no mistake about it, this childhood, as you will learn from the letters, is without a trace of infantilism. It readily shoulders responsibilities for the simple reason it knows the Father wants them shouldered. It carries them fearlessly and discharges them effectively; for the consciousness that the Father is watching and is always present gives one a courage nothing can daunt and a confidence nothing will ever shake.

It is painful to note that men will readily accept and gladly adopt almost any other attitude toward God save this proper one of being His child. Dom Gerard knew he was laboring in that vineyard owned by the Almighty, but no matter under what guise he looked at God, he always saw the possessive sparkle of Paternity in the eyes that looked back at him. That is Christian adulthood — and there is no other. For a Christian is mature only when he knows that he is kin to Divinity; that he is a child whose Father is the only omnipotent and everlasting Lord.

It was this maturity which gave Dom Gerard the integrated character which was so marked and unmistakable in him. What makes an integrated person? What marks a man as integral? What is integrity? A man is integrated when he is whole. But no man is whole until he is holy. That is the first meaning of the Anglo-Saxon word *halig*. That is the ultimate meaning of our modern word *integration*.

Reading these letters you will see how consistent this young monk was. Realizing that he was a son of God, and knowing that his Father was all-holy, he saw the sense and the connoted obligation in the dictum "like father, like son." Applying that to his daily living brought him back to the original and precise definition of man as "a person who can be filled with God" — for God is Holiness.

Religion, man's relation to God, is the very core of life, the base as well as the crown of man's character, the very substance of proper living. This young monk saw that when life's ultimate audit is made, no man can be called a real man unless he has become a holy man.

Catechisms define faith accurately. Manuals of dogmatic theology analyze faith faultlessly. But only letters like these of Dom Gerard to his sisters and brothers are capable of showing you the reality, the vitality, the intimacy with God, which is the essence of this wondrous gift which can be merited by no man, but which is offered to every man coming into this world, as St. John intimates in the very Prologue to his Gospel. For they show you first that while faith will beget deep feelings, stir powerful emotions, and even inflame passions, it is never a matter of mere feelings, emotions, or passions. Faith may demand profoundest thought and spur one on to sublimest thinking, but it is never a mere matter of thought or thinking. Faith is a face-to-face encounter with the all-holy Trinity, or it is sheer travesty; it is man's freely willed response to the eternally free and deliberate decree of Divinity to reveal Itself in all Its Three-Personed splendor in and through Christ Jesus.

Letters like these of Dom Gerard will enable you to see that what we call Divine Providence is, in all reality, the two hands of God our Father — the right hand of Wisdom and the left hand of Love — stretched out to help us every split second of our existence; and to help us on, not only to success, but to triumph. With an eloquence born of personal experience, he will convince you that no matter what those hands hold — be it bodily affliction, strain for mind, crushing frustration, humiliating defeat, veritable human heartbreak — it is always a gift of Wisdom and a token of Love.

When John Bernard McGinley arrived at Gethsemani Dom Edmond Obrecht was abbot of the monastery. Dom Edmond Obrecht was a stern master of men and a stronghanded molder of monks. Every postulant and novice at Gethsemani was soon made to realize that he had entered what was then considered the strictest and most austere Order in the Church, and that he was living in one of the strictest and most austere houses of that Order.

Edmond Obrecht, who had made his own novitiate at La Grande Trappe, universally recognized as the house of greatest asceticism in all Europe, had been commissioned by Rome to come to Gethsemani to save the abbey by his strong and steady hand. It is no matter for wonder then that Gethsemani became La Grande Trappe of the New World, noted even in Europe for its austerity in food, clothing, housing, and for its strict observance of the Rule. The somewhat shy and retiring young McGinley could have met his Waterloo early — most likely would have — had he not been blessed with a virile belief in God as Father who plans, protects, and provides, coupled with at least a subconscious knowledge that "all things work together unto good for those who love him" (Rom. 8:28).

Young McGinley has been typed as "somewhat shy and retiring." There was a ready explanation for this shyness: he labored under a difficult impediment in his speech, a defect cited as the reason for his choice of Gethsemani, after he had traveled all the way from Minnesota to New Jersey to join the Paulists.

Some might suppose that the Trappist silence would preclude every possibility for embarrassment to anyone who suffered from a speech impediment. The novice master of the Paulists thought so; that is why he endorsed McGinley's choice. But, most likely, he never adverted to the fact that these silent monks of La Trappe use their voices more, perhaps, than any other group of men in the world. At that time the Trappists used to spend from seven to eight hours a day, every day, chanting the praises of God. Any stutterer might find difficulty in attempting that. As for embarrassment, there are occasions when every monk in choir is called upon to do some solo work. Besides, each choir monk is supposed to take his turn reading at table and in chapter; and every candidate for the priesthood has to go through a long training in Philosophy and Theology, during which he will often be called upon to recite in class. Finally, every Trappist priest has to preach to the assembled community some time during the year, has to participate in theological conferences at least once a month, and has to sing the Conventual Mass when his turn comes. Obviously, there are plenty of opportunities for embarrassment to any stutterer.

Many a postulant and novice got his first close-up look at Gerard McGinley when he saw him seated in the middle of the chapter room trying to read to the community just before the Compline hour. His stutter was painfully pronounced. It was only late in his life that he was allowed to attempt to read in the refectory; and it was only in his last years of life that the defect all but disappeared. But more arresting than the disturbing stutter was the utter unconcern of the stutterer, at least externally. Both as scholastic and young priest, his public reading was an ordeal, not only for him but for his listeners as well. Yet he always appeared as the least perturbed in the entire assembly. The explanation lies not in any feigned indifference or pretended carelessness about the impression he made, for, true child of God that he was, Gerard McGinley was always keenly anxious to make the best impression possible. The explanation is given in more than one of these letters which show this man to have been needle-sharp in his consciousness of the sadly neglected truth that God is God, and that, consequently, nothing can happen that is not somehow part of God's plan.

Had John Bernard McGinley had no speech defect, most likely he would never have so much as thought of Gethsemani. Had he never come to Gethsemani, the world would have been poorer for never having met a person and a personality who proves so conclusively that Galilee is not twenty centuries past; that Nazareth is in America; that the light Christ came to kindle can be seen aflame in the eyes of those of our contemporaries who, like Gerard, merit the name of Christians.

In letter after letter Dom Gerard gives some sister or brother of his the two major premises of a syllogism whose conclusion always reads: "Therefore, no matter what happens, it is somehow willed or permitted by God — and willed or permitted by Him for my good."

That is the doctrine technically known as "Holy Abandonment." It is as logical, and as irrefutable, as the multiplication table; but when it comes to the living of life, not even our best mathematicians are that logical. Yet, until we master that logic, we will never be able to lead life with that peace of mind which should characterize every true Christian. It was late January, 1926, when John Bernard McGinley arrived at Gethsemani. In the very first letter he wrote from the enclosure he exclaimed: "If you could be here for a day you would wonder why God stays out in the world at all when there is a place like this where He might come and be honored in a way that must be most pleasing to Him." That is not exact theology by any means, but it is precision-sighting on the very heart of the target — at which every Trappist should aim: "To honor God in a way most pleasing to

Him." Easter Sunday of that year saw this young man clothed in the Trappist habit and his canonical novitiate officially begun. Two years later, on an Easter Sunday again, he completed that novitiate by pronouncing simple vows. Ordinarily, another Easter Sunday, or thereabouts, in 1931, should have witnessed his solemn profession. Yet the records show that 1931 went by and more than half of 1932 had passed before he was allowed to pay God those solemn vows. Such a delay, in any man but one completely abandoned to God's good pleasure, could easily produce depression, but Frater Gerard cheerfully passes it off with the cliché: "Man proposes; God disposes."

Were there any doubt about that fact, the letters concerning his ordination would shatter it. For he had told his nun-sister that "the Lord has been drawing me to the altar since the age of five." In the spring of 1931 he was writing to the same sister about the possibility of his being priested in 1932. But then in May, 1933, he writes: "About three weeks ago the doctor thought it would be well for me to discontinue my studies for some time and get a little more outdoor exercise. . . . So for the rest, we are in the good hands of the Lord who only permits what is for our best, even when we do not see it. . . . For religious, disappointments and crosses are never a surprise. . . . It is for your sakes I am sorry. . . ." On the threshold of his life's accomplishment, and he is forbidden to step across.

In the correspondence for 1933 and 1934 you will look in vain for self-pity or discontent; for this man knew that by waiting he was doing God's will; and, for him, that was as perfect a sacrifice as he could then be offering.

At this critical juncture in his life perhaps no better description of his soul's attitude can be found than in those lines of Jeremias which say:

"The Lord is my portion, said my soul:
therefore will I wait for him.
"The Lord is good to them that hope in him,
to the soul that seeketh him.
"It is good to wait with silence
for the salvation of God.

"It is good for a man,
when he hath borne the yoke from his youth.
"He shall sit solitary, and hold his peace:
because he hath taken it upon himself" (Lam. 3:24–28).

God had shaped this monk's soul along these saintly lines by sending from Belgium in 1927 a retired abbot whose every heart-beat was an act of abandonment. The Right Reverend Dom Vital Klinski was the instrument God used early in Gerard's life; for this retired abbot became the most popular confessor at Gethsemani, and his one doctrine and devotion was that of Holy Abandonment.

To make security doubly secure God had the general chapter and the Most Reverend Father General of the Order highly endorse a book by the Right Reverend Dom Vital Lehodey, Abbot Emeritus of the Trappist Abbey of Notre Dame de Grace, at Bricquebec, in France. It was titled *Le Saint Abandon* and has since become something of a classic on the subject. It was translated into English in 1934, and so great was the enthusiasm it kindled that, for a time, it looked as if "Holy Abandonment" would become *the* Trappist devotion and doctrine.

But Holy Abandonment was not the ruling doctrine of Dom Gerard's life and the devotion that finally shaped his soul. Letter after letter tells of the Little Flower and that "Little Way" of hers which brings such big results. In 1928, at his simple profession, Gerard had taken her as his "counsellor and consolation." In 1955, after visiting Lisieux, he was heard to say: "Now I am ready to die." That he lived on intimate terms with the young Carmelite in the almost three decades that stretch between is eloquently attested by these letters.

Dom Edmond Obrecht was another man that God used to shape the soul of the young Trappist. This man had one time severely reprimanded his prior, Father Mary Frederic Dunne, for having the *Autobiography of a Soul* read to the community while he was away. He wanted men saints as models for his monks, rugged oaks, not "little flowers." But when Dom Obrecht returned from Europe in 1926, some six weeks after John Bernard McGinley had entered Gethsemani, he was burning with enthusiasm for this same Little Flower. He had the *Autobiography of a Soul* read again to his monks — and commented on it frequently. For he was convinced that it was Soeur Thérèse of the Child Jesus who had miraculously cured him of his heart disease the moment he stepped into the sacristy at Lisieux, thanks to the last permission granted by Pius XI for anyone to enter the cloister at Carmel.

In 1927 this burly Alsatian was officially adopted into the Martin family by a document drawn up and signed by the three living sisters of Soeur Thérèse, to which they had appended the words "*Et Moi Aussi*" — "Me, too" — which they had clipped from Thérèse's writings. From then on, Gethsemani's monks heard more about the Little Flower than about any other saint on the Church's calendar.

But perhaps a deeper influence upon the young monk was that from the monastery's prior, Father Mary Frederic Dunne. This man had a truer appreciation of Thérèse's worth than that enjoyed by Dom Obrecht, for his was a clearer understanding of Christ's Gospel and the teachings of St. John and St. Paul. Father Frederic had immediately seen that the "Little Way" was not new; nor was it in any way little. He recognized it as God's way of presenting the age-old doctrine in a manner that would appeal to the modern world. In what Thérèse had written he heard that command of Christ implicit in those words to His Apostles: "Unless you become as little children . . ." Frederic saw clearly that the "Little Way" was identical with the way of St. Paul and the way of St. John, for it was the only way, the way of love.

In Dom Obrecht's many absences from the monastery it was Father Frederic who gave the chapter talks to the community. He gave that "Little Way" which demands so much virile strength and whole-souled love. Hence, if God used Dom Obrecht to take young McGinley through the purgative way, He used Father Frederic to take him on into the illuminative and even to the unitive way.

The paternal tenderness of God is seen in giving the young monk as guide a man as gentle, yet as steady and strong as was Frederic Dunne. For Gerard McGinley was going to be taken into the depths of that dark mystery which is God's providence. No one could teach him better than Mary Frederic Dunne.

Wise in the ways of God, when he saw this young monk held up for solemn profession, then advised to interrupt his studies just after receiving the subdeaconate, Father Frederic felt sure that here was a chosen soul. He quietly but steadily guided the young monk.

Edmond Obrecht died in January of 1935. In February of the same year Mary Frederic Dunne was elected to succeed him. Two months later he had Gerard McGinley kneeling beneath the outstretched hand of a bishop who was calling down the Holy Spirit and imparting the order of deaconate. Before that year was out, the patient, long-suffering Gerard was ordained a priest of God.

The letter he wrote home after that Christmas is one of the shortest in this collection. Yet it reveals, as perhaps no other, the man, the monk, the priest, and the contemplative. It is a page that can be read as purest Christian humanism. It stands as proof that before any man can make real progress in the spiritual life, before his soul can take on anything like definite shape, he must get very near to Christ in His Passion; he must share suffering with Jesus, and make complete personal sacrifice of self in Christ. For it seems evident that God the Father has but one form for the shaping of souls, the one He used for His only Son on Golgotha. Every Christian, if he will be a true Christian, must become cruciform. Gerard had done that. That is why God had made him priest.

But ordination marked only the end of the canonically prescribed studies; it did not mark the end of God's soul-sculpturing. Once again that pattern of the Father is discernible. Golgotha came after Gethsemani; the mental anguish was followed by the physical Passion. Father Gerard's fatigue had left by the time he had received sacred orders, so God bestowed His next blessing on the body which had just been chrismed in those priestly anointings. The newly ordained was found to have diabetes. He was treated expertly enough, but he was never cured. For almost twenty years Father Gerard needed, and took, the maximum dosage of insulin a man can tolerate. As with one afflicted with diabetes, his physical energy did not increase; but the disease played no small part in developing his saintly character and greatly increasing the energy of his soul.

It was because of this affliction, as much as anything else, that

Dom Frederic appointed the young priest to the post of monastery infirmarian. As is to be expected, a Trappist monastery is not a place where the human body is pampered. Hence, the infirmary is used little except by those old men who have given their lives to God and become truly decrepit in His service. But that meant daily contact for the young priest with battle-scarred veterans; men worn out by the long campaigning, who were now awaiting the final roll call; souls who were filled with God and alive with longing to see Him face to face. Gerard's devotion to Holy Abandonment and the "Little Way" increased quantitatively and qualitatively; for he saw what they could and did mean in the lives of these aged monks.

As infirmarian, he also learned what death really is. Death in a Trappist infirmary flings wide the gates of heaven for every monk who assists at the deathbed; for the liturgy summons angels and archangels, saint upon saint, the Virgin Mother herself, then calls upon the Father, Son, and Holy Spirit with an earnestness and intimate directness that cannot be denied. There is splendor surrounding the passing of any monk to that Reward — who is our God; and it can only be described by the adjective "heavenly." It is no cause for wonder that Father Gerard grew while infirmarian. But the point is that God used a bodily affliction to get him to that post.

Dom Mary Frederic Dunne was an abbot in the best sense of that word. He was a watchful father to whom the immortal soul of every son of his was almost as holy as the consecrated Species. He actually saw in them what he saw in the transubstantiated Host. Hence, his prime concern was always for their betterment. But he had a large monastery to administer, too. So he was ever on the *qui vive* to spot talent and to see that it was used for God. Yet he was adamant on the principle of never sending a boy on a man's errand; for Dom Frederic, in his almost half century of observing, had noted that no man is made a true Trappist by two years' novitiate, nor even by three years of simple profession. He was convinced that before the blood of Robert, Alberic, and Stephen, the founders of the Cistercians, was coursing in any man's veins; before the spirit of Bernard, Aelred, and Amadeus, those propagators of the Order, was breathing in a man's whole body; before the fire of a Largentier, de Rancé, or a de Lestrange, those restorers of the Observance, was burning steadily in the center of a man's being, he must have lived at least a dozen years in the Trappist regime, and lived them generously. "*Natura non fit per saltus*," he would laughingly say — "Nature does nothing by leaps and bounds" — then add: "*Neque supernatura*" — "Neither does supernature." So when Dom Frederic appointed Father Gerard guest master one year, then retreat master the next year, only to follow that with the appointment of master of the professed lay brothers, you can be sure that he felt that the complete change of mind and heart and will which marks a monk as definitely mature had been accomplished.

Gerard had had no contacts with those whom he had come to call "outsiders" for over fifteen years. So a touch of shyness and an occasional stutter reappeared during the first few months of his term as guest master. But soon that mysterious aura which he carried about him was having its effect on the guests, and had them seeking him out not only as confidant, but as confessor. A newer gentleness came over and came out from Gerard as his soul broadened and his human sympathy, which was ever tinged with something divine, deepened.

From his letters it is most evident that the assignment he liked best was that as master of the professed lay brothers. That is understandable enough; he felt that it was here among these wrinkled, bent, quiet-moving men, many of them golden jubilarians, that he found the truest Trappists and some of the highest contemplatives. It was here, perhaps more than anywhere else, he saw and appreciated the virtue which is the characteristic virtue of the true Trappist: simplicity.

Dom Frederic's final and fullest act of approval came when he appointed Father Gerard master of the lay brother novices. *Spes gregis*, "the hope of the flock," is the name given to novices. They are the future monks, the ones who will lift the monastery to newer heights of holiness or drag it down to that mediocrity which St. John tells us disgusts God. Hence, the man appointed to train them should be — and under Dom Frederic was — among the very best monks in the community. He has to be the *forma gregis*, the true and perfect pattern for the flock.

That Dom Frederic knew his man, and that the Little Flower was still generous with "roses," was evident when the lay brother novitiate not only improved in tone, but became so enriched with new recruits, that for the first time in the almost one hundred years of Gethsemani the lay brother novices outnumbered the novices for the choir. Father Gerard attributed it all to the Little Flower, but there were those who saw that no little of it was due to the radiant personality of the kind and gentle master, Father Gerard.

When Dom Frederic was so suddenly taken to God in the late summer of 1948, and Dom James Fox elected to succeed him, the first, and among the most important, moves made by the new abbot was to shift Father Gerard from the lay brothers' novitiate to that for the choir monks. Again the tone was lifted, and the applicants flocked in. That is why Dom James was enabled, in the very first year of his abbacy, to complete Dom Frederic's plan for a foundation in South Carolina and turn his eyes to the outlines the same Dom Frederic had left for a house in New York.

By this time Father Gerard had had wide and varied experience with souls — from those ready to go to God in the infirmary, to those just beginning to seek God in the novitiates. But as yet he had had no administrative training or experience. So, to fit him for what lay ahead, God had Dom James appoint him prior of Gethsemani in late 1949.

In an ordinary Trappist monastery the office of prior would not burden the incumbent too heavily with responsibility for the administration of the house. But in 1949 Gethsemani was anything but an ordinary Trappist monastery; for from 1936, when Dom Mary Frederic Dunne became abbot, Gethsemani had grown steadily. In the middle of World War II it was so overcrowded that Dom Frederic had had to make the first Trappist foundation from an American house in the history of the Order. After that war the influx of ex-GI's was so phenomenal that a second foundation had had to be made. And when he died, Dom Frederic had all but completed plans for two other houses. Hence, when Dom James took over the government of America's protoabbey he had three actual houses and two potential ones to care for. That entailed no little travel and many absences from the motherhouse, and in the abbot's many absences, Gerard, as prior, had to assume responsibility for the running of Gethsemani.

Dom James and Father Gerard had been novices together. Gerard had followed James in the offices of infirmarian, retreat master, master of the professed lay brothers, and finally, prior. They understood one another thoroughly and worked together exceptionally well. Hence, it was something of a sacrifice when the Abbot of Gethsemani confided to his intimate in the late summer of 1949 that he wanted him to be the superior for the foundation to be made in New York.

While he remained prior of the still growing Gethsemani, he had to prepare everything that would be needed in the new house at Genesee. The poise and pace that marked the man during the next two years are accounted for in these letters; for no one could bear the mental and physical stresses inescapable in his position had he not a mind keen for ready assent to whatever God asked and a body that would shrink from labor no more than did Christ. Abandonment, the "Little Way," and great-souled, virile love were seen rolled in one.

The simply curious are going to be disappointed when they find in these letters so few details of the day-to-day existence of the monk behind his cloistering walls. As Frater, Father, and Dom, Gerard makes hardly a reference to the externals of the Trappist life. Yet even the simply curious can hardly fail to see in these same letters what is the essence of Trappist living; for Gerard is always talking about the liturgy.

Here again he shatters definitions, destroys common concepts, but gives insight into the very soul of the liturgy and the liturgical life. What has already been said of the Trappist life must be repeated about the liturgical life: it is not something; it is Someone. Christ is our liturgy and our liturgist. In the Cenacle and on Golgotha he carried out the public worship due to God — and He did it in our name. Now we, with Him, and in Him, and through Him, carry on that same liturgy that the Father may have the loving adoration and the adoring love that is His due from all His children, and that sinners might be saved.

The Mass, of course, is the heart of the liturgy and the heart of the Trappists' day. But it is not only when in choir or while assisting at Mass that the monk allows Christ to live in him, and that he strives to live in Christ. It is all day and every day that this liturgy goes on. In Gerard McGinley at Gethsemani Christ lived His Bethlehem, Egypt, Nazareth, and Jerusalem just as really as He had lived them two thousand years ago in the Holy Land. Here was the same painful poverty and deep obscurity; here the same hard manual labor and the slow years of quiet growth far from the rush of the political, economic, and even the wide social world. Here, too, were experienced the same misunderstanding by the world, its scorn, and ultimate rejection. Christ lived again, and lived as liturgist, in this boy from Minnesota who became pliable clay in the hands of God the Father. It was this liturgy which made this monk a contemplative and led him into the fully contemplative life.

Shortly before his death, Pius XII described the essence of that life as "the adherence of the intellect and heart to God." That description, in almost those identical words, will be found again and again in these letters, as Dom Gerard endeavors to show some brother or sister the way to perfect peace, truest happiness, and ultimate glory.

But the lesson of all lessons that this young monk teaches is the one which says that sanctity is easy. To one of his family he wrote: "To become a saint is easy; for we need only to have one desire: that of giving pleasure to Jesus in all things."

What Dom Gerard teaches is that sanctity is easy in the sense that, in itself, it is nowise complex, nor need its prosecution ever be complicated. Its essence is simplicity; its substance, sincerity. Sanctity is easy. He proved it by his life.

We need to know that a person is a capacity for God; that a personality is a radiance of God; that true liberty is the freedom of the sons of God; that real maturity is childhood under God; that proper integration is intimate union with God; and that Divine Providence really means life in the very hands of God.

Dom Gerard McGinley was not only a man of God; he was a veritable manifestation of God. His letters can bring our God-consciousness to the point of kindling in us a veritable passion to become what God made us to be: wholly human because so definitely divine.

FATHER M. RAYMOND, O.C.S.O.

Gethsemani
Easter, 1959

IMPORTANT DAYS IN THE LIFE OF JOHN BERNARD MCGINLEY

(ABBOT GERARD McGINLEY, O.C.S.O.)

April 21, 1906	Born on the family homestead near Baldwin, Wisconsin.
May 20, 1906	Baptized at the parish church, El Paso, Wisconsin, in the diocese of La Crosse.
September, 1911	Entered Tydalen Elementary School. Later attended Wildwood.
September, 1919	Enrolled at St. Mary's Academy, Altoona, Wisconsin.
September, 1921	Transferred to Cretin High School, St. Paul, Minnesota, where he was graduated in June, 1923.
September, 1923	Studied at Nazareth Hall, St. Paul, Minnesota.
September, 1925	Went to the Paulist Novitiate, Oak Ridge, New Jersey.
January 29, 1926	Entered Our Lady of Gethsemani, Trappist, Kentucky.
July 2, 1932	Professed as a Trappist.
December 21, 1935	Ordained to the priesthood at Gethsemani.
August 22, 1949	Appointed the first superior of the projected monastery at Piffard, New York.
October 13, 1953	Elected the first abbot of Our Lady of the Genesee, Piffard, New York.
September 19, 1955	Died at Dijon, France, while attending a world meeting of Trappist-Cistercian abbots.
October 6, 1955	Buried at Our Lady of the Genesee, Piffard, New York.

I

NEW LIFE AT OUR LADY OF GETHSEMANI, TRAPPIST, KENTUCKY

IT WAS a cold day in January, 1926, when Bernard McGinley wrote to his brothers and sisters (his parents were no longer living) that he was going off to the Trappist monastery in Kentucky, a place almost unheard of in the early twentieth century. The boy had studied for a few months with the Paulists and had rather suddenly decided to transfer to the Trappists. When his sister heard of his decision, she wrote to the novice master, Reverend Robert A. Skinner, at the Paulist novitiate in Oak Ridge, New Jersey, to ask his opinion of the transfer. His reply, dated February 8, 1926, read as follows:

"Before your letter reached here, Bernard had already arrived at the monastery of Our Lady of Gethsemani, Trappist, Kentucky. . . . The reason which impelled Bernard to leave us was primarily his defect in speech. He had made a very earnest effort since coming here to overcome his stutter, but after four months he was no better, and he found that his efforts to control his speech were reacting unfavorably upon his spiritual life. When this became evident to him, his mind turned toward the contemplative life and to the Trappists, of whom he heard before coming to us. He seemed to have a special attraction to them.

"With my permission he wrote asking about their life and whether he could be admitted. He received a very encouraging letter from the Abbot and a booklet describing the life. The booklet only seemed to confirm what he already knew about the life and furnished him with some new details. It is true that the Trappist life is quite austere. I think, however, that there is nothing about it beyond Bernard's ability or strength to carry out.

"He did not want to go back into the world again and so went directly to Kentucky from here. There is a two-year novitiate; so if he finds the life does not suit him, he can leave it any time during those two years.

"Unless he becomes cured of the stuttering, he would never be able to follow the career of a priest in the active life. So having an attraction for the contemplative life anyway, he has done well, I think, to seek the Trappists, where he can devote his life to work and prayer and so gain many souls for God, more, probably, than he would have been able to do as a priest of an active Order.

"I think his family need feel no apprehensions about Bernard. I would recommend that you assure him of your sympathy with him in his move and encourage him to try it; and if he does not like it, assure him of a glad reception back to his family."

That explanation satisfied the family.

On the way to Gethsemani, Bernard wrote: "You may regard your little brother as a prisoner, but a prisoner of love. Don't forget me in your prayers and ask Jesus to fill my heart with His love and even fill it to overflowing that I might give some to others. . . . I am very happy because it has happened that God has willed to call me to such a high state. I am the happiest person on this train."

Bernard was still happier when he reached the monastery where the monks chanted the Divine Office. In the family circle at home he had known the joy of music and song, a remote preparation for the chant of a monastic choir. Occasionally he wrote to William, Agnes (Mrs. Edward Lavelle), Sylvester, Mary Evangeline (Mrs. Joseph Fell), Anastasia (Sister Myron) McGinley, his sisters and brothers, telling them of his way of life;

and these letters and the group letters are included in this collection.

As soon as he reached the monastery, Bernard wrote to his sister, Sister Myron, O.S.B., at St. Joseph, Minnesota, to tell her about his new surroundings.

Trappist, Kentucky
January 31, 1926

Dear Sister Myron,

Your little brother is within the walls of the Trappist monastery, but although a Trappist at heart, he has as yet not any exterior signs of a regular Trappist. I am a postulant now, but within a few days I shall enter the novitiate — this lasts two years. . . .

If you could but be here for one day, you would wonder why God stays out in the world at all when there is a place like this where He might come and be honored in a way which must be most pleasing to Him. The Divine Office is chanted in the large church by about forty masculine voices. All the singing which I have ever heard in churches has always been spoiled by a majority of high and seemingly superfluous feminine voices.

High above the main altar is a statue of Our Lady, and every evening the lay brothers and choir religious gather before the altar. The statue is then lit up by colored lights, and all chant the *Salve Regina*. It is the most solemn and impressive service that I have seen. We have a solemn High Mass every morning.

No, Sister Myron, you can't become a Trappist even though you would like to. Now there is also a hard side to this life of the Trappist, and it is made light only by the grace of God. So although you cannot become a Trappist, still you can send your delegate by praying for me. Father Master told me that the devil is here also, and how he hates a Trappist monk. He gets a very poor reception around here, and this makes him all the more furious, so pray God to beat him for me as I am not able to combat him myself.

I don't know if I can write you again before receiving the

habit, but if I don't, remember that I want you to ask Jesus to allow one spark from His fire of love to fall upon my heart and enkindle in it a fire of love that will burn forever, until one day it might become so strong that it will sever my soul from my body.

Father Master was just up and told me that tomorrow I would be allowed to eat dinner and go to choir with the religious. He also told me that I must keep my secular clothes for two or three weeks. Father Master entered here when he was sixteen and is not dead yet, to use his own words. So unless God wishes to use some other means, the life itself will not cause my death, at least not before I am ordained. St. Bernard assures us that a Trappist is undergoing a slow martyrdom, and what religious doesn't sigh for a death with Christ.

Don't worry about me because I now weigh very nearly 170 pounds, which is more than I have ever weighed in my life.

I have been eating with a White Father from Africa, who is making a retreat here. He left this morning for Africa. He came to America on a begging tour, as he called it. Don't forget to tell the Sisters to pray for him because he told me of his experiences. . . . They surely have a much harder time than we ever imagine.

I will remember you at the *Salve Regina.*

Bernard

Bernard's brothers were very close to him. William had given him a home after the death of his parents; Sylvester took care of his affairs. To the latter, who acted as his guardian, he wrote an apologetic letter begging pardon for failing to wait for permission before going to Gethsemani. In order to make things right, Bernard invited his brother to make a retreat at the monastery, secretly hoping, no doubt, that his single brother would like Gethsemani and remain there for the rest of his life.

Trappist P.O., Ky.
Feb. 7, 1926

Dear Syl:

I wish to ask pardon for playing the fugitive, for I must appear as one to you. I received a letter from Father Skinner about a day after I came, and I was quite surprised not to find a message from you. He told me that you wrote him in order to be more certain that I was not doing what I have done too hastily.

I asked you to wire your consent, as Father thought for my peace of mind that it would be best to leave within a short time. He then asked me if I thought you would consent; and I, probably somewhat presumptuously, assured him that you would, so I wrote to the Trappists that I would be there about the middle of the following week. I waited an extra day before starting that I might receive your message, but it did not come, so Father thought I might go on without it as I knew you would consent.

Trappists do not live an easy life, it is true, but it does not, however, mean a sudden death when one enters the Order. A brother just died yesterday; he has been in the Order about fifty years — and he is not a great exception.

You need not have any fear for my care because I am living very well. I am not allowed to fast, and I receive extra sleep. Father Master is my private "call boy," calling me just in time to get to church for Matins. I can see you any time — of course, you must come here. I would like you to make a retreat, either private or with the K.C.'s who come here during the summer months, if I remember rightly. My profession will not be until after two years of novitiate.

We do not write letters during Lent unless it is necessary. Lent is not far off so my next letter will be about Easter.

My ship has been tossed about much during my short life, but it fills me with great joy when I think of my next step — heaven. Father Superior said this morning in chapter that there is but one thing necessary — the salvation of our souls. I have often heard this before, but it never impressed me as it did this morning, probably because I was looking at the wasted body of our dead brother. When we are ready to die and waiting for the last breath of life, we are not going to say, "Oh, world, why did I not amass more riches and have more enjoyment while with you?" but rather, "Why did I as much as even look at you?" Oh, deceitful world, where is your consolation? Then is the time that your works for God will be your only consolation. When one comes to die . . . one will say, "Why wasn't I a saint?"

There are eighty men here who have entered by the narrow gate. We spend almost eight hours each day in the presence of the Blessed Sacrament. I am permitted to chant the Divine Office in choir, and I often offer this up for you and the rest of the family, especially for father and mother. This is the greatest prayer of the Church. A saint has said that "Monks do what the angels in heaven do."

I hear about three and sometimes four Masses every morning. This morning I went to the church while the private Masses were being said, and there was an almost continual ringing of bells for about five minutes. One priest at the elevation of the Mass, another at the Communion, etc. Then I thought of what a saint said, "One Mass gives more glory to God than can all the angels in heaven for all eternity."

I am surely happy to be here. Pray for me, for sometimes there are little things that are somewhat hard, and I need the grace of God.

Brother Bernard

The "little things that are somewhat hard" were never referred to again in Bernard's letters.

At the monastery his meals were simple: a large bowl of nourishing soup and another one of vegetables, some fruit if the monastery had any, and as much dark mysterious whole wheat bread as he needed. Once in a while the community received a treat of candy or a few nuts at table. While the Rule of St. Benedict makes exceptions for the sick, the monks have no meat, fish, or eggs on their daily menu. Part of the year they have neither milk nor cheese.

Bernard might have minded the monastic silence. But he could speak to the abbot, his spiritual father, at any time. Then, too, he could confer with his confessor, any priest of his choice, to whom he might like to go for counsel and forgiveness. But he would never be allowed to recreate with his confreres.

The boy knew that he would be obliged to give away practically everything he possessed. He could keep paper, pen, and a few personal items in an open box in the scriptorium, but nothing else.

His clothing, too, would be simple: a white habit and a black scapular, a cowl (white choir cloak), a black leather girdle, and shoes.

It was on Easter Sunday in 1926 that Bernard was clothed in the ancient Cistercian habit and given a new name, Gerard. His letters from the novitiate gave the family a new insight into the monastic life.

December 20, 1926

Dear Syl:

The happy season of Christmas so near at hand makes one naturally feel a little of that joy which even those not of the faith experience by reason of the general rejoicing about them. You probably experience this external joy to its fullest extent in Chicago, for every store window must remind you of the holy season. I am sure that you make use of those external signs to enkindle your spirit that you might receive the Christ Child on Christmas morning with a heart full of love and adoration for the Divine Infant.

Our joy, of course, is purely spiritual, and although the hills are covered with Christmas trees, they will not be decorated with baseball bats, teddy bears and the like. I hope that God will decorate them Himself with a little snow. We have none now, although it is cold enough to snow, and it looks as if it will tonight. We have more than all this, for we have all the consolation the Church offers at this season in the Divine Office and in the Holy Mass.

I asked Reverend Father if I might ask you down, and he told me to have you come down for a little retreat. I should have asked you to come down for Christmas . . . but most of the day would be taken up in church (and if you were here a couple of the brothers would miss some of the exercises taking care of you). I am sure you would want them to be at peace with the Child Jesus on such a great feast day. Reverend Father told me to have you come down for New Year's day as that is also a feast of sermon, and Reverend Father said he will celebrate pontifical High Mass.* I am sure you haven't an opportunity of assisting at one often.

Be sure to write us when you are coming because we have to meet you, for Gethsemani, about the size of Wildwood, has not many taxi drivers waiting for passengers. I think you can get a train right out here without stopping at Louisville. Anyway, I guess that "Information" in Chicago will know that better than I, although "Information" gave me some wrong information when going to New York.

If it is impossible to come on New Year's for some reason or other, there is another feast of sermon on the sixth of January. Let us know when you will come. Plan on a little retreat, as I am sure if you don't need one, at least it will help you a great lot to revive the life of the spirit. If you have gone up to Bill's for Christmas, this letter will hardly reach you before New Year's, but anyway, God will arrange all things well.

Our family this year will be more distant than perhaps ever before. Yet we must be thankful that God leaves us together on earth to serve Him a few short years more. When one gets out of the world so he can look into it, he sees with Shakespeare that life is but a stage where men come and play their part and retire. Well, let's play our part well that we might please the Divine Infant and His Mother who are the noble personages always sitting in the box seat where they can watch us more perfectly.

I will write a letter to the rest of the family within a few days, as Reverend Father will by then have given out general permission.

I have no gold or silver to give you for a Christmas present, but you can be sure that at Communion and during the Offices on that day, I will not forget to pray to Jesus for you. And I pray Him to give the unction to my desire when I say that with my whole heart and in the name of Little Jesus and Mary, I wish you a truly Merry Christmas and a happy New Year.

Your brother in the heart of Christ,
frater Gerard

---

* In his monastery an abbot may use a throne and celebrate liturgical functions "pontifically," with rites similar to those of a bishop.

Gerard's brothers were most curious about the life of a Trappist. They resolved to find out by paying their young brother a surprise visit.

When they reached Gethsemani, it was dusk. They walked down the long path that led to the gatehouse. All was quiet and peaceful. Not a stir from the monks. The only sound they heard was an occasional song of a vesper sparrow. Arriving at the entrance, they looked in vain for a doorbell. They knocked loudly on the door. No response. One of the boys spotted a wooden cross suspended from a wire high above the door. Scaling the wall, he pulled the cross, and to his amazement, all the bells of the monastery seemed to ring out. They wondered about their next move. Should they go back to Louisville for the night and try again the next morning? Bravely they stood at the door.

After what seemed to them an interminable wait, a smiling brother appeared at the door and graciously invited them into the gatehouse. Though they arrived after hours, they were received hospitably and kindly. It was the last time they ever visited the monastery unannounced.

After they visited with Frater Gerard, the brothers were convinced that though the life was rugged, it would make a man out of their young brother.

When the time of his profession approached, Gerard invited his brother Syl to visit the monastery again, knowing well that instructions for guests would not need repetition this time.

January 6, 1928

Dear Syl—

I have permission to write four letters home, for Reverend Father doesn't like those circular letters which have to go from New York to St. Paul and back to Honolulu. One religious here gets one twenty pages long. All of the family are religious but one, and there are about nine in the family. You might remember him; he is the one Reverend Father sent to cut off the limb of the apple tree when we were at the barn.

We spent a happy Christmas, with two pontifical High Masses, one at midnight. We have two abbots here now; one is from

Holland. He has resigned and is going to stay here the rest of his life.

It was cold here Christmas, but we had no snow. I always like snow for Christmas, but we were in church most of the day so it didn't take anything away from the joy of the feast.

As I said, we were happy until about 2:30 in the afternoon when we got word, just when going to Vespers, that Brother Francis died. He was with us all day; received Communion at midnight, and served Reverend Father's dinner. About one o'clock he told Reverend Father he wasn't feeling very well and asked if he might lie down. He went up to the infirmary and the brother examined him and gave him a few pills. Within an hour he was found dead. He, of course, received conditional extreme unction as soon as he was found, but Reverend Father assured us he was well prepared. He was a model of charity, and charity covers a multitude of sins. I have heard of sudden deaths, but I have never seen one. It surely brings before one's mind the necessity of being ever prepared.

Today we are celebrating the feast of the Epiphany. I hope you went to church. It is not a holy day of obligation, although it is in some countries. But it is the day on which we were called to the faith and deserves special regard on that account.

I asked Reverend Father about [your] coming down for Easter. He said sometimes we get the grip around that time, but he will gladly have you come. But I will let you know for certain about three weeks before. You can plan on coming, however. I finish my novitiate on the fourth of April, and Easter is on the eighth; so, if accepted, I will make my profession on that day. The simple (for three years) profession takes place in the chapter room, and therefore you could not see the actual profession. The ceremonies are very simple for the first profession. The solemn takes place in the church with great solemnity. Please pray for me that I may be accepted if it is God's will, and especially ask that He might take my life rather than that I sully my second baptismal robe.

We have spring weather here, or rather, early fall weather, for everything is dry and not at all cold. We had zero weather for Christmas but no snow.

Reverend Father was at general chapter this year and also at

Rome. He had an interview with the Holy Father. He talked for three hours with the sisters of St. Thérèse, he being a special friend of Mother Agnes of Jesus, the little mother of the Little Flower, and superioress of the convent. I told Stasia [Sister Myron] all about the visit; she may send you the letter.

They are building a basilica in honor of the Little Saint of the shower of roses. Reverend Father is gathering a collection to send to Mother Agnes of Jesus, and he asked us to recommend the good work to our relations. . . . You might as well be the collector for them all. I don't think it will be necessary to engage a box in the trust bank, however.

I will write to Ev, or rather, would you write to her, and ask her if she has any devotion to the Little Flower; and if she has, it surely would be an excellent way to gain a special rose, to give something towards the basilica. If she has no devotion to her, then tell her to give something that she might gain some devotion to the saint who promised to shower down roses from heaven. When she gets to heaven she can look down and see her name engraved in the altar of the basilica by the hand of Little Thérèse — and her companions will envy (if such a feeling is possible in heaven) her for doing so much good on earth with such little effort. I will write a letter to Ev later and thank her for her offering. Tell her I am not unmindful of her Christmas bouquet.

When you write to Stasia, would you ask her if she has a relic of the Little Flower. Reverend Father told me he would give me one to send to her if she has none. Tell her to write that I might send it before Lent. I got a piece of her brown habit for Christmas. Some got a piece of her coffin.

You ought to go down to visit her shrine in Chicago. We read about it in the refectory last week in the book, *The Living Sisters of the Little Flower*, by Dolan.

May Jesus grant you a joyful New Year.

frater Gerard

II

LIFE AT GETHSEMANI AS A PROFESSED MONK

GERARD made his first profession of vows on Easter Sunday, 1928, when he promised obedience, poverty, chastity, conversion of morals, and stability. By the last-named vow, he promised to remain at Gethsemani until his death unless he happened to be sent to help establish a new monastery at another place.

He was willing to wear the tonsure, also known as a monastic crown, around his head as an external sign of his desire to alienate himself from the spirit and style of the world. He wanted to love men, not their worldly ways. That his interest in the affairs of the family never waned is indicated in the following letters, one to his brother Sylvester, whose work entailed considerable traveling, and another to his sister Agnes, her husband Edward, and their children, Kathleen, Ann, and John, who were then living on a farm in Wisconsin.

Novitiate
May 8, 1930

Dear Syl:

You are having a fine time aren't you — assisting at a dog race in Mexico, and the next day, dining with a Virginian judge. . . .

I indeed envy you in your travels, viewing so widely the works of God and man. I content myself with saying after Little Thérèse, "In Jesus I have the hills, the valleys, the streams, the velvety heather upon the plain." Perhaps you have learned by this time through experience what the prophet said long ago. "The eye is not filled with seeing nor ear with hearing." Solomon said that he had seen everything under the sun and found all to be vanity and vexation of spirit.

If you go to Washington, D. C., be sure to visit the Catholic University. . . .

I am glad that you are coming here on your way back to Chicago. Be sure to let me know some time before [you arrive].

Reverend Father* has not been feeling well the last few days. His heart is especially bad today. Outside of a little dizziness — a semi-natural state, you may say — this spring, I have been very well.

During this beautiful month of Mary I am sure you are offering her some little proof of your love for her. Doubtless you say your rosary daily, but at least during this month you should say it without fail. . . . Let us be assured that if we are devout to Mary, we need have no fear. May she obtain for you all the graces you need.

frater Mary Gerard

Dec. 26, 1930

Dear Sister [Agnes] and Edward —

Your very kind letters added much to my Christmas joys. I have not received the box as yet, but Christmas mail is often delayed. (The box just arrived.)

I hear from all sides that you have three blooming roses at your house, delighting all who draw near by the fragrance of their virtues. You have a very delicate charge but also a very joyous and

* Abbot Edmond Obrecht.

meritorious one. For as they are trained now, so they will be all their lives. If they are taught now the law of charity, to love God above all and all that He has created for His sake, this will grow upon them and form a noble character. They will do what is right because they are attracted towards Goodness. The way of fright and fear often develops a nervous disposition and occasions many disasters in the soul. The Little Flower often committed a fault, but immediately she ran and kissed her mother, promising not to do it again, and all was forgotten.

If I had been told some little anecdotes of the lives of the saints in place of those of the little red hen — finally ending by a great bear jumping out and scaring me stiff, often causing terror in my dreams — I believe I would practice virtue now with greater ease than I do.

Developing piety — always simple and true — in souls is one of the best and the only way to foster a good disposition. Of course, to do all this . . . you must set them an example for . . . example draws one after it. Very often I used to look at Mother when saying the rosary, and immediately I would kneel upright as she was.

I am very happy that Kathleen prays for me daily, and I trust very much in her prayers. Can our Lord refuse her anything? You can tell her that I remember her daily, too, at Communion. I always ask our Lord to bless Bill and Veronica and their family; Ag and Ed and their family, etc. You were all very personally near my heart on Christmas night as I received the new born Babe into my soul. I am sure He smiled benignly upon you and granted many petitions of your heart. I hope you receive Communion as often as you can, for It is so beneficial to us and so pleasing to Jesus that we do so.

The box of sweets just arrived . . . and I wish to express my hearty thanks to Kathleen and Ann with all the effusions of my heart. I have a picture of Kathleen when she had two teeth. I suppose she has a whole family of them now.

Speaking of pictures, I wonder if you have a picture of Mother, that one taken in St. Paul. She has an apron on. I believe that is her best. Then, too, if you have a good one of Stasia as a nun, I would be very pleased if you would send it — not framed or anything, of course; just little snapshots.

Sometimes when I don't know Syl's address, I send the letter to you. Please don't return it, telling me that you are not Syl. Of course, I will only do this when I have nothing bad to say about you.

Just gazing out the window, my eye falls upon a very picturesque landscape. We are in the midst of the Kentucky knolls, and to the west of the monastery they form a circular gigantic hedge sloping down into the valley below. This hedge was covered with snow last evening, and the weather being warm, it clung to the branches of the fir trees, forming a most charming panorama — nature, ermine-bedecked, in its sprightly clothing of festive joy. The valley remains dark and sombre, not having been visited by winter's chosen mantle of crystal white. The surrounding country is apt to inspire in the mind of a poet most lofty sentiments and imaginative flights of celestial grandeur. But as I am not sufficiently fledged to soar to those giddy heights, I will content myself by saying: "Great is the Lord and greatly to be praised, who alone doth wonderful things."

You doubtless feel the so-called hard times which are passing over the entire world. You may be thankful that you are on a farm where there is always plenty of work even though the recompense is somewhat lessened. We daily receive many requests for prayers that a husband might get work to supply the necessities of his family. Yet while during this Christmastide we hear the voice of the angel saying, "Fear not, for behold to you is born a Savior," how can we but believe that this same Savior will assuage our present fear and cause that peace and joy which He has brought upon the earth, to again reign in our hearts. The Christmas wish which I implore for you all is that Bethlehem's Child might be with you in joy and sorrow, 'til united in heaven in the eternal tomorrow.

Your affectionate brother in Christ,
fr. Mary Gerard

As the time of his ordination approached, Gerard's family recalled his early attraction to the priesthood. They remembered his climbing on the highest chair when he returned from High

Mass, and, on tiptoe, trying to match note for note the high tenor of the pastor's Ite, Missa est. *One time when he was questioned as to what he wanted to be when he grew up, he asked the practical question: "How much does a priest get?"*

In his letters to his sister, the young monk wrote at length about the happenings in the monastic family at Gethsemani.

March 25, 1931

Dear Sister Myron:

I find it indeed providential that I am beginning this letter to you on this holy day, Good Friday, at this time when the words of our Lord, "Father, forgive them," are still echoing through your soul. I say this, for I feel the need of pardon, and since we are Christians in so far as we imitate our Lord with whom there is mercy, I look eagerly and confidently to you for a heart-sprung, *Vade in pace.*

I trust Syl has explained to you my dilatory disposition so you will not think any longer that Gerard's heart is one of stone rather than of flesh, even if he doesn't write. So again, Sister Myron, pardon, won't you?

Our winter blasts have given way to spring's gentle zephyrs of life and warmth. Nature around here is quite inspiring at times. Sometimes I attempt to describe it, but I seem to drown all in the ocean of my inability. . . . Just last evening after the night office, I gazed out upon the slumbering panorama, all modestly concealed under a veil of silvery grey with which during the silence and quiet of the night it had been mantled with Jack Frost's hoary hand. This seemed decorated and embellished as it lay dazzling in the sheen of a silvery moon.

The morning sun rising over the valleys and towering knolls caused the spring verdure to glow in brilliant sprays as a sea of many-colored gems. But within a few hours, this charming paradise was denuded of its borrowed garb and metamorphosed into a new creation where the entire scene again resumed its dull, drab hues of early spring.

This Easter dawn will be somewhat shrouded by a cloud of sorrow which has not entirely disappeared from our hearts, at least not from mine. I sent you a notice of the death to which I refer. I will tell you the story in a few words. About the first of March our little Frater Thaddeus was seemingly just as strong and active as any member of the house. One morning he had a hemorrhage; two more followed that same day, and one during the night. Of course this made him very weak. He contracted pneumonia . . . Father Master spent the night with him, but left him about Mass time with sure hope that he would recover. When Father ended Mass, he heard that he was dead.

This little frater had a great devotion to St. Thérèse, and just before he expired, he opened his big blue eyes and died with those very words of St. Thérèse on his lips: "My God, I love You." I had the happiness of assisting Father Infirmarian in giving him Communion each morning at about two a.m. He died about an hour after Communion.

We were to make our profession together after Easter, if received by the community. We see again, "Man proposes, and God disposes."

Speaking of my profession, I probably will make it now about the middle of May. I will try to write you a line to let you know the exact date. In the meantime, please remember me occasionally, won't you?

You spoke of my ordination. Well, *Deo Volente*, it could take place a year from this spring. I will probably receive minor orders shortly after my solemn profession.

Is little Sister Annella* still continuing her graces? Did you hear of this Therese Neumann? What do you think of her? . . .

I wished to say a few words about this glorious season, but the liturgy is *one* and equally inspiring, so let us just remain in the heart of the Church and thus in the hearts of Jesus and Mary in whom I will be found.

Your brother,
fr. M. Gerard

---

* Sister Annella Zervas, O.S.B., whose unusual death attracted a large number of people.

Trappist, Kentucky
Aug. 13, 1932

My dearest Sister [Myron],

It seems that nearly half of my life has swept away since my last lines to you. Indeed, it has nearly done so, judging from important events. For what event in life can be more momentous than the act of one's solemn profession? Our Lord well knows with what magnitude I regarded it both as to its obligations and its privileges.

What may I not expect from Him who assures us that we can not make a greater act of love than to lay down our life for our Friend. "I dispose to you a kingdom." "You shall possess eternal life." "Enter into the joy of our Lord." All these rapturous greetings our dearest Friend bids us await.

When will all this take place? Very soon. "I come quickly," says our Lord. It only remains to fight amid the shadows of faith until the victory be ours — or rather until the Divine Eagle swoops down to draw us out from the midst of the arena. For those who follow the Lamb through heaven's realms are those who have come out of great tribulation, and who have remained with Him in His temptations.

The truths of faith are encouraging and uplifting and continually fill the soul with expectant joy.

I will tell you about the ceremonies, although your profession is, I suppose, more or less the same.

First of all, my retreat before the event was somewhat disturbed by business affairs; however, the morning finally arrived and about twenty degrees cooler than the preceding day. This was a special gift of heaven — doubtless the Little Flower had her hand in it, at Mary's command, however.

In the morning my soul was filled with quiet peace, free from thrilling joy as well as from oppressive dryness.

After chapter, Tierce, and procession, Holy Mass began. At the gospel we, Frater Eugene and myself, accompanied by Father Prior, entered the sanctuary. There we listened to a sermon or exhortation addressed to us by one of the Fathers. Then turning toward Reverend Father, after this short address, we made known our resolutions of keeping the Rule in its entirety. Then kneeling, turned toward the altar, the choir sang the *Veni Creator.*

Having invoked Him who contains all love of heaven and earth, we sang our formulas. I, being senior, sang ours first. Then having signed it, we placed it on the altar, which we kissed. We returned and sang together the *Suscipe*, and proceeded to embrace every choir religious in the Church, saying "*Ora pro me, Pater,*" to which each responded, "May the Lord keep your going in and your going out." The *Te Deum* was then sung, and Mass continued.

During Sext which followed Mass, Reverend Father called me out and told me that two brothers and two sisters were here. You can imagine how surprised I was. I had expected Ev and Joe . . . but I had no idea that Bill and Agnes would come. Then as long as they stayed, I took dinner and supper with them. Ev and Joe left the next morning; Ag and Bill, Monday morning. They said that they would be sure to arrange for your coming next year.

About two weeks after our profession, Reverend Father announced in chapter that two of us would be made (or ordained) subdeacons soon. It was to take place last Saturday, but the Bishop thought it better to wait until about November, for I need three more months of study, according to Canon Law.

You see . . . the priesthood is in sight. With regard to my studies, I don't do too badly, but as for virtues, I face a yawning void. As I draw near to the sanctuary, I feel more and more drawn to imitate those saints who have shrunk from the priestly dignity. On the other hand, our Lord has been drawing me on from the age of five. Then, too, I have consulted many of my spiritual directors during life on the point, and every time it was a positive, "By all means, go on for the priesthood." While recalling those words of our Lord to His ministers, "He who hears you, hears Me," my heart fills with untold joy, for it is Jesus Himself who invites me to approach. So with entire abandon to His Divine Heart, I will not even look at myself, but keeping as closely united to Him as possible, I will try to imitate more closely His every thought, word, and deed.

Since even the angels would be unworthy to be ordained priests, what should not poor man do to try to lessen the distance, at least, from that purity of heart which it is possible to attain?

So, please, Sister Myron, have a very special prayer for me during the coming year that I might not pass over those great events of my life with hardly any preparation. I catch my pen running on because of its facile nature, beyond due bounds, so the remainder of my letter will be mere sententious remarks. . . .

May our Lord grant you success in your studies, advancing in grace before God and man.

Prayers and affection,
fr. M. Gerard

From childhood, Gerard loved to observe his surroundings, particularly the color and beauty in sunrises and sunsets. In his letters home the family understood his idea of relaxing: noticing and enjoying God's created wonders around him.

Feb. 2, 1932

Dear Syl,

This is the feast of the Purification of the Blessed Virgin Mary or Candlemas day, as it is better known. We had a profession this morning, a very fine young man who seems to have the aureola of glory already encircling his worthy brow, hovering there—trembling with the desire to rest there forever.

Grandfather, I believe, said that we should have half of our food and half of our hay on this blessed day. Well, I believe we have, for we have been having very mild weather here, vacillating between spring and winter. While we rejoice in our Lord's providence, I still fear that Kentucky is in danger of the Gospel's anathema, for it is neither hot nor cold. However, as a redeeming feature, the beauty of the heavens is most ravishing at times. The other morning while eating mixt* I was attracted by the sheen of a bloody sunrise. . . . Wishing to enjoy this providential splendor with greater leisure and ampler view, I walked out, after making a visit and inviting our Lord to enjoy it with me. The

* Breakfast of six ounces of bread and coffee.

ruffled clouds mantling the eastern horizon were aflame as it were — an intense fire emitting rays varied and brilliant, yet soft. . . . There were oases of blue cropping through the blazing mass, tempering and adding beauty to the picture. From the heart of this fiery sea, blood streams were sent out along the low clouds, capping the undulating knolls in the distance. The sunset that evening was one of soft silvery white, so beautiful that I cannot, will not, attempt to describe it.

Please remember me in your prayers during this lenten season. I will have you near at heart in our austerities and prayers.

Your brother in Corde Jesu,
fr. M. Gerard

On June 11, 1932, before making solemn vows, Gerard wrote:

. . . As I am now nearing the eve of the greatest day of my life, I would ask that you kindly be united with me in my preparation.

I say it is a great day, for it is the most solemn act that a man can make here below. It has two sides — it is a great glory, but also a great obligation. It seems to me to be the greatest act of love which man can make to God. For our Lord Himself has said: 'Greater love than this no man hath that he lay down his life for his friend.' He has also said, 'He that hates his life in this world shall keep it unto life everlasting.'

The fathers of the Church regard the solemn vows as a second baptism, so what joy would it not be were our Lord to grant me to die on that blessed day and enter heaven without delay?

In 1932, Mary Evangeline, Gerard's sister, sent him an announcement of her approaching marriage. In his letter of felicitation to her, he included a quotation he had read:

"A good wife is like a fresh flower, always in bloom;
and a wrangling wife is like a leaky roof, continually dripping through."

He told her of one couple that had the practice of sitting down and writing out their grievances whenever one looked cross at the other party. He concluded his letter in his casual, humorous way:

You spoke about driving out here, but you wanted me to be very frank with you, so I shall be. Only men are allowed in the monastery proper; there are large guest quarters for them. Ladies may visit the church. We have a ladies' apartment at the gatehouse about twenty steps from the monastery, but it is not very serviceable in winter, for it must be heated by a stove. . . . So you see, if you planned on staying overnight, the summertime would be more ideal. . . . I might mention that you will find me bereft of my disheveled hair and with a beard. So don't ask to see Bernard when Frater Gerard comes.

In the next series of letters, the young Trappist unfolds his way of love to the family. While there was scarcely any evidence that he was suffering, his brothers and sisters knew well what he was undergoing and read between the lines that his cross was great. His ordination would be delayed because of his poor health. From childhood he looked for God's will; by now he accepted it from the loving hands of his Father. But suppose the family would be disappointed about the delay in his ordination? That was his one concern.

Trappist P.O., Ky.
December 25, 1932

Dear Syl,

The great day . . . which for centuries has caused the whole world to shake from pole to pole with joy and glee is drawing to its close. Pontifical Vespers which will take place in an hour or two will bestow the last benediction to crown its grace-laden moments.

As you know, after having retired at five o'clock on Christmas eve, we rise again at nine o'clock and sing the Divine Office until eleven-thirty, and at that time the Office is especially beautiful. We then have free time until twelve, when midnight Mass begins. Our pontifical functions are beautiful — more so than those in the Cathedral in St. Paul.

Last night was especially sweet for me, for I received Communion nearer to the crib than ever before. I say *crib;* I mean the *tabernacle* — the true crib. This was granted to me because I had the privilege of ministering to the Mass as subdeacon. Does this surprise you? Yes, I was ordained subdeacon Saturday, December 17. I will probably be ordained deacon on Saturday before Passion Sunday. Reverend Father told me that I could tell you that, God willing, I will be ordained to the priesthood about the end of June. These are great privileges indeed — privileges of which the very angels would be unworthy. You see then, Syl, what need I, a poor sinful creature, have of your good prayers. Many of the greatest saints have refused to be raised to so holy a dignity — and I? Yet, when one acts according to direction and obedience, one acts most wisely. And thus it is I presume to approach the altar, but not without trembling for my poverty and weakness. But "In Thee, O Lord, I trust." Would you please, Syl, from time to time say a "Hail Mary" that our Lord would take my life shortly after ordination rather than ever let me offend Him? For what could I desire more? Our Lord will have bestowed upon me His highest privileges — to be a contemplative solemnly professed religious and a priest forever. How angelic the life of a Trappist religious should be! But when I behold so much self-love, self-will, and weakness in myself, I recall that the mercy of God is above all His works. So if we try to remain as a little child before Him, He will not be displeased with us despite our failings. For a loving mother is not displeased with her child because of his involuntary or even voluntary faults of which he repents.

Christmas always conjures up before my mind scenes and thoughts of home. I behold the entire family around the glowing fire with Mother in our midst — the victrola sounding forth a loved melody; Ev's Christmas tree in the corner with presents strewn around, the Christmas dinner with the turkey fair and fat, the giving of the presents in the evening . . . and a host of other memories on which I fondly dwell. Again further back, I recall those Christmases spent in union with the Farrell family,* when all was joy without alloy. Sweet days to return no more. Indeed, we have not here a lasting city, but there is one to come.

When we consider how our dear Lord came into and passed

* The Farrells were relatives.

out of this life, we are persuaded that the greatest joy and truest joy on earth is the joy of suffering. He who had every grace and quality possible for our human nature to bear lived thirty years in obscurity; and just upon arriving at the fullness of manhood gave Himself over to be mocked and spit upon, and put to death — the death of the cross. . . .

Be assured, Syl, that you are often in my prayerful thoughts, and with all the fervor of my heart do I wish you a truly holy Christmas.

May little Jesus bless you.

fr. M. Gerard, O.C.S.O.

Trappist P.O., Ky.
Dec. 30, 1932

Dear Ag and Ed:

Christmas has come and gone, but its gift of joy and good will linger in our hearts like the echo of distant music. Doubtless in our way of judging, it was not the merriest Christmas in history; yet perhaps in the sight of God all was well.

I don't believe that I told you that on December 17, I was ordained subdeacon. You can suppose how the usual heavenly peace, which Christmas eve inspires, was greatly enhanced in my soul, when, in silent expectation and the night in the middle of its course, just before the *Gloria in excelsis* of the angels, when the Eternal Word leaped down from the bosom of the Father to be born again in our midst, I sang in the sight of the angels my second epistle at solemn High Mass in pontifical rite. Next year, God willing, I will have the privilege of celebrating three Masses both on Christmas and on All Souls' Day. What is less inviting — I will have to preach a sermon on All Saints' Day.

Tell Kathleen that I think with joy on her "Hail Mary," especially in the immediate preparation for my priesthood. I believe that you said her first Communion would be soon. Our Lord cannot deny her anything on that day. So I will form my intention now. We were just reading of the Little Flower's preparation for Communion. She prepared in a special manner during one month preceding by making several sacrifices and about fifty acts of love each day — "Sweet Jesus, I love You." I like "Sweet Heart of Jesus, be my love." I like it best.

How sweet was the family of the Little Flower, yet so simple, so ordinary. Nothing of gloom or exaggerated piety, but a truly Christian life — happy and full of love for God and for each other. Her mother worked very hard all during her life amid suffering and sorrow. I wish that you could read this beautiful book that we are reading in the refectory.

I asked the prayers of the community for Edward Riley; may he rest in peace. For us, let us be prepared, for we know not the day nor the hour. Souls have revealed that they would come back to life and endure all suffering till the end of time to be permitted to make one act of love for God — such is the reward. We can make many of those each day without interfering with our duties at all. How a good life will console our last moments! I am greatly moved by the thought that the moment of death will fix our lot in heaven for eternity. We know that no act of ours, even though good in itself, will be rewarded without a supernatural intention. That is why it is so good to make an offering of all our prayers, works, and sufferings of the day in our morning prayers. It is well, if we can, to renew it by a mere thought during the day, but even the initial act will meet with approval.

I have made a consecration of myself to the Blessed Virgin, so before my principal action — even sleep — I say: "I wish to do this with Mary's faith, hope and charity and for her intention." This includes everything, for Mary never allows herself to be outdone in love and liberality. But if I fall, since Mary is our Mother, my very faults make her love me more. It is so good to be near to Mary; she is so sweet, maternal, and so powerful. For her prayers are commands, since they are addressed to her Son. Finally, if we persevere in the true devotion to Mary, our salvation is assured. I hope you have the good practice of saying the rosary during Lent. If you obtain Mary's blessing for your family, you need have no worry for their future. . . .

I had many things to tell you, but two pages* seem very short unless one writes purely news.

I wish to say especially that we had several happy days of late. Reverend Father celebrated his eightieth birthday on Novem-

* Young monks were apparently kept to two pages when writing letters.

ber thirteenth. We had a pleasant little feast day of the event. I told you that Reverend Father was in Europe this fall; while there he visited the three sisters of St. Thérèse. He had a two-hour talk with them in a family circle. He said Mass in the infirmary where the Saint died. His health is quite good of late.

The flu is hovering about — may you be protected under Mary's blue mantle.

May your New Year be most holy, happy, and rich in graces.

Your brother in Jesus,
fr. M. Gerard

Abbey of Gethsemani
May 21, 1933

Dear Ev and Joe,

This is the first letter I have written since I wrote you last February. So you see you are both first and the last — much like our Lord — the beginning and the end. . . .

I am most grateful for your good prayers during March. Our dearest Mother has laid them up among her heart's treasures to reward you in eternity, and to bestow grace upon me in seasonable aid.

Well, Ev, despite all those fervent prayers that were offered for me, and the good intentions of Reverend Father and the Bishop, I am not yet ordained deacon. "Man proposes, but God disposes." A few weeks after I wrote you, Reverend Father and two religious had a most serious accident. The condition of the driver and Reverend Father was very precarious for a long time. [At the time] there was little hope for the other party with whom they collided, but he is now improving. To make known the peril of it all, it will be sufficient to say that the dealer would not give five cents for the car after the collision. Those injured are practically recovered now.

So the above is the reason of the first delay, but now my health is delaying it again. About three weeks ago the doctor thought it would be well for me to discontinue my studies for some time and get a little more outdoor exercise. So I am not studying now, but I go out to hoe the garden, etc., a couple of hours in the morning and in the evening — the regular rule of the priests. It is not a case of phthisis. . . . A little too much mental application. It is quite ordinary in seminaries, for the studies bring on a nervous condition at times. I take a little more sleep and a side dish or so in the refectory. So for the rest we are in the good hands of our dear Lord who only permits what is for our best even when we do not see it.

For religious, disappointments and crosses are never a surprise; then besides I am quite indifferent as to the time of ordination. I would like to be a priest before I die, but I have often wished to die soon after being ordained. For this will perfect my consecration to our Lord.

It is more for your sakes that I am sorry for the delay — but I trust no one has planned too much.

It is a great source of peace amid the changes and reverses of life if we make these two principles our own: (1) Nothing happens but [what] God either wills or permits. (2) Everything that He permits is for my good, if I accept it. As one author remarked, if we had this deeply implanted in our souls there would be miles and miles of smiles, for nothing could trouble us.

Will you please write to Syl and tell him that the ordination will not take place. I will write Bill, and he can tell Ag.

Our Kentucky knolls are all leafed out and flowing with delights, smiling back their thanks to the Giver of the abundance of moisture with which they are bedewed this spring.

We are at present having our regular visitation, that is, the abbot of our motherhouse in France is here to see that all is well. . . .

May God bless you and Joe abundantly.

Affectionately in Jesus and Mary,
fr. M. Gerard

On September 30, 1933, Gerard wrote to his sister, explaining that in spite of hardships, St. Thérèse claims it is easy to become a saint.

I am beginning this on the eve of the Little Flower's heavenly birthday, or that of her precious death. I feel sure that tomorrow will witness an avalanche of heavenly-kissed roses — graces for saints and sinners alike. She promised that she would not only look down, but really come down. To those whom she loved dearest — her own sisters — she promised graces indeed, but in the form of crosses. For she said that suffering was her sole desire here below. So suffering must be a true good. We know that if we desire eternal life we must keep the commandments, but this necessarily entails suffering. For when our feelings are hurt, our first impulse is to return evil for evil, and our pride, our self-love is excruciated when we impose silence and gentleness on ourselves. Thus it always implies suffering to curb our evil inclinations of which the heart of man is so full.

Despite all this, the Little Flower assures us that to become a saint is easy, for we need only to have one desire — that of giving pleasure to Jesus in all things. When we fail, a little aspiration of love corrects all.

If we are not saints, I fear we will have very little excuse on the general reckoning day. We have ample means in the sacraments and the communion of saints. We need only to perform as perfectly as we can the duties of our state in life, accept all that happens to us, good and bad, and all out of love and a desire to please Him. This very desire will bring into our souls a spirit of recollection and prayer, or little sighs of love. . . .

In 1933, during the height of the Depression, Frater Gerard wrote to one of his brothers:

"I notice, as you undoubtedly will, too, that the poverty of the times has found its way into our stationery box." *He added however:* "The less we have in this world, the more we will have in the kingdom of heaven."

In his Christmas letters, Gerard told the family of the new hope he experienced in studying the Church's liturgy.

Our Lady of Gethsemani
Dec. 23, 1933

My very dear sister [Eva]:

I take up my Christmas pen — but lo, it is still Advent time. How shall I sing the canticle of the Lord, as it were, in a strange land? . . .

When you read these lines the Church will have already proclaimed with silvery voice, yet trembling with emotion: "Jesus the Son of God is born in Bethlehem of Juda." And the midnight angels shall have trumpeted forth, both earth and heavenward, that soul-enrapturing anthem: "*Gloria in excelsis Deo* and peace on earth." What have we to do, Eva, but be silent, adore and love. Let us draw near to Mary and gaze into those heaven-lit eyes of her divine Babe. Are they not the eyes of Love? For God is Love. There is something so entrancingly peaceful about this mystery of Bethlehem that its memory causes one's whole being to vibrate, as it were, with sweet harmonies of heavenly music.

Alas, Eva, I must stay our pen lest I consume our two pages by the exulting and heaven-bent thoughts to which the feast gives rise. I cease, too, for well do I know that your own soul is filled with floods of light and love upon this day which from childhood — as I recall — you have cherished and kept with sweet jubilee. . . .

However, if our more mature years bring with them more stern realities, we must never forget that heaven was, and is, won by the cross alone. We are inclined to forget this, when looking upon, and partaking of the joys of the crib. Yet Bethlehem can only be rightly understood when studied in the shadow of the cross. We learn so much from a prayerful study of Bethlehem. What greater lesson can this silent, helpless Babe teach than the lesson of perfect trust and entire abandon? We know, Eva, that whether in the world or in the cloister, we must strive to be more perfect, to be saints. Of course, our perfection is in direct proportion of our love. There are many roads leading to the apex of the mountain of love. The way of abandonment and love — for love hopeth all things — is such a sweet way. There are few asperities in its path, or if there be any, they are softened by confidence and love. Abandonment rests simply upon two infallible truths applied to each event of our lives. First: *Nothing happens but what God either wills or permits.* Secondly: *Everything that he permits is for my good if I accept it patiently and lovingly.* It is true that it takes years and years for this principle to sink deep into the marrow of our being. So we must seek God's will alone in all that happens to us, and in all that is asked of us by the duties of our state: get up — because it is God's will; go to work — because God expects it of us. Do all that we do because it is in conformity with the will of God. So by this abandonment we intend to do God's will in all, thus to please Him always. You know, Eva, that our merit depends on our supernatural intention. A general intention, said each morning, will suffice, but the more particular and the more often it is renewed, of course, the more meritorious it is.

Perhaps you have a better one, but I like this little intention: "I wish to do all my actions today in union with all the love of heaven and earth, and with Mary's faith, hope and charity and for her intentions." This endows each act with the highest possible supernatural value.

Well, Ev, as you see, I have run off on a tangent. I notice, too, that the end of the page is in sight, so the rest must necessarily be cut. Unlike you, I do not see the "coldness"* in your gift. Indeed, I know of no warmer gift in these impecunious times upon which the whole world has fallen. Your gift fills me with gladness, for in it I recognize not only your affection and thoughtful kindness, but moreover I feel and am sure that the gift benefits you more than it does me. For it is more blessed to give than to receive. Then, too, by your gifts you constitute yourself a benefactor. I do not have enough space to enumerate all the prayers and Masses we offer for living and dead benefactors. You know that according to our Lord, the widow's mite was more than all the rest. So if, as to sum, you are not the greatest benefactor, nevertheless, I am sure you share largely in the prayers because of your good disposition.

Reverend Father remains about the same; his side bothers him at times. We just came out of retreat last week. The sum of the

* Ev had sent her brother a check.

news of the monastery is: we are preparing our hearts for the birth of our Saviour. . . .

Give a warm greeting to Joe, to whom as to you, I wish a most Merry Christmas and thrice Happy New Year.

May the Divine Infant come and visit your souls in peace, and may all heaven be attentive to the least desire of your hearts. This is my prayer for you on my knees before the crib.

In Jesus and Mary,
fr. M. Gerard, O.C.S.O.

Dec. 27, 1933

My dear Sister Myron:

May the little Jesus caress your soul in peace and sweet jubilee. Since you say the Divine Office, your soul at this season could hardly be otherwise than aglow, set on fire, as it must be, with those inspired words of light and love. I sort of wonder at times why my soul does not fly off into ecstasy when singing some of those antiphons and hymns of heaven. The reading of the *Liturgical Year*, by Gueranger, translated from the French by Dom Shepherd, O.S.B., is for me a great help to enter more deeply into the spirit of the Office and Mass. The Little Flower speaks of it in her autobiography. . . .

I am stopped short here, Sister. . . . Just while in silence and solitude I was pushing our pen noiselessly along these somewhat fractured lines, Father Prior rushed in and hastily bade me put paper and pen away and follow him. So . . . I followed. Then suddenly he told me that Mr. and Mrs. Fell were at the gate. Well, you know the rest. They stayed about an hour. It was most kind of them to drop in. They were at Louisville, and it is about fifty miles out to Gethsemani. They were here last June, too, you know, and stayed two or three hours. Doubtless they are trying to avoid ever hearing, "I was in prison and you visited Me not." In their charity they find joy in giving me joy. Ev looks very well, and Joe, too. I like him very much.

Now see here, my good Sister Myron, your Christmas letter

was entirely too short. If your health is the "why" of it, I willingly grant you . . . indulgence. . . . I deeply sympathize with you in this visitation common to all the fallen sons of Adam. However, in a more supernatural spirit, I congratulate you upon being found worthy of this fond embrace of your crucified Love. For surely if there were a more certain sign of His love, our Lord would have bestowed it upon His saints. But no, He ever remains the same crucified Jesus, and scourges every son whom He receives. Be careful to regard it as coming from Him and unite it to all His sufferings and those of His saints.

Personally, I am a miser when it comes to heavenly goods, so desiring to clothe my acts with as great supernatural value as possible. I like to perform them "in union with all the love of heaven and earth, and with Mary's faith, hope, and charity, and for her intentions."

I remember in your letter last August that you said you were greatly impressed by the retreat master's words: "When you love, you do not suffer." Well, those are words of St. Augustine, but mark that St. Augustine continues and says, "or if you suffer, you love the very suffering." This latter is the case with most of the saints, especially the Little Flower, whom I call my spiritual counselor and consoler. Her sister Marie is going down fast. Reverend Father receives a letter from Mother Agnes quite often. He reads them in chapter. They are so spiritually sweet — poetical, too. Just one instance: last time she wished that the Little Flower would impress a kiss upon Reverend Father, in the manner in which the angels kiss each other. To listen to her letters is like hobnobbing with the saints.

Reverend Father is not well these days. He has a paralytic side which fills me with anxiety. He is along in the eighties, so a little sickness for him is dangerous. . . .

Thanks very much for the picture of Sister Annella. How is devotion to her progressing? We just received the life of a holy nun of our Order the other day. Her motto was: "See God's will in everything, everywhere, and always."

Please do not keep too keen an eye on the rhetorical value of these lines. . . . I place the thoughts as my heart dictates them. . . .

I am not studying yet, though I am slowly improving.

Letters are so short — for me . . . that I cherish the hope that some day I'll be able to have a little talk with you. Of course, this means that you'll have to come here.

May the Little Jesus embrace you tenderly.

fr. M. Gerard, O.C.S.O.

The illness of Dom Edmond Obrecht, the abbot of Gethsemani, was serious in 1934. The strength of the eighty-two-year-old superior was gradually waning. In his letters home, Frater Gerard kept the family informed of the abbot's condition.

April 7, 1934

Dear Syl:

. . . I am glad that you are busy, for idleness is the enemy of the soul. What is "C.W.A."? "Christian (or Catholic) Welfare Association"? "Can't Work Atall," perhaps. You see, our Kentucky knolls with their leafy canopies do not admit of such beneficent societies, encumbered and conserved as they are by their somniferous and quiet-loving inhabitants — namely, a few stray mules grazing lazily about some bootlegger's camp ensconced under some protruding rock. . . .

As for news of the monastery, we are building an addition to our enclosure. About two months' work.

The trees are well leafed out, and the varied flowers send forth most ravishing perfumes. The sweet trill of the many-feathered birds . . . echo through the valleys. . . . I sigh: "Poor Syl beholds only the rugged brick or stony walls towering up to shut out the very . . . heavens. And he listens to the din of passing traffic!" Perhaps my threnody is too sombre, and you no longer dream of Wildwood's charms.

Reverend Father is not at all well these days. He has varicose veins, and a bad heart. . . . His mental faculties remain vigorously active.

Abbot Dom Gerard McGinley, o.c.s.o.

Father Gerard as a young monk at Our Lady of Gethsemani, Trappist, Kentucky.

Dom Gerard examining the Chandler property for a desirable site on which to build the monastery.

The first monastery built by the monks at Piffard, New York.

The monks gathering straw from the Genesee River bottom land.

The first monastic refectory at Our Lady of the Genesee Abbey. The monks listen to reading as they refresh their bodies.

The monastic community at Our Lady of the Genesee, Piffard, New York.

Abbot Gerard McGinley, O.C.S.O. (center, carrying crosier) at the Cathedral of the Sacred Heart, Rochester, New York, November 9, 1953, the day he was blessed as abbot.

The General Chapter, 1955, Citeaux, France. *This is the last picture of Abbot Gerard* (*third row, second from left*).

As for Frater Gerard, I am quite well but have not resumed my studies as yet. When will I? Whenever our dear Lord sees fit, for there is nothing that can resist His will.

I was glad to see in your letter that you leave our Lord to do your planning of the future for you. Of course we know we must not throw the oars overboard and let things go. But just do what we think is right, what we think He wishes us to do, and then let Him fill in the details and even to draw glory from our mistakes and failures. For the last word on the road to heaven is "Begin again." Our falls will not hurt us, provided we do not lie there. For how good is Jesus, and how He loves us! We are His beloved little children — little children, indeed, no matter how gigantic our stature or brilliant our minds. We are mere nothings before Him, yet most beloved through Jesus' merits.

I had many little things I wished to speak about, but, when speaking to you, I find two sheets glide by quickly.

You know, Syl, that the merit of our actions is derived from our intention. A natural end — a natural action; a supernatural intention in any form gives the act supernatural value. This is sound theology. I find it consoling, and doubtless you would, too, to offer all I do, think, or say in union with all the love of heaven and earth, and this with Mary's dispositions and for her intentions. I cannot conceive a higher morning intention.

We are celebrating a great day of prayer in union with the Carmel of Lisieux — the golden jubilee of St. Thérèse's first Communion, and Mother Agnes's profession. The chasuble at Mass was made by Celine — a gift to Reverend Father.

Affectionately,
fr. M. Gerard

Our Lady of Gethsemani
December 24, 1934

Dear Ev and Joe:

The year's cycle, containing its weal and woe of human affairs, has again brought around the ever-ancient and ever-new consoling and sanctifying mystery of Christmas. Its glad advent is rung in by every frosted bell, tingling with trembling sound. In rapt awe we listen to their chimes as in soft waves they glide over our Kentucky knolls and float lingeringly on the still air of the valleys. They seem as faint echoes of the angelic thunders of song as once they swept and do still sweep around the crib of the Babe (for eternity has no time) in gorgeous oceans of melodious sound, causing earth to tune in with heaven and cheer Eve's mourning children with the thrill of its becoming bells.

Well, I do not wish to resume this letter in waves of airy poetry (as someone calls poetry), but if any day tends to give wings to one's thoughts and to bear them away on zephyrs of sweet harmony, surely it is this day when the bloom of God's love flashes over the earth with its radiance which bursts forth from the never-setting sun of Bethlehem's Crib.

However, in the midst of all this glad and merry melody which almost naturally inundates our souls, there sounds forth, all too loudly, unmistakable notes of an impending threnody with its sobering air.

Reverend Father . . . received extreme unction on his birthday, November 13. . . . since then he has been confined to bed, gradually sinking under the weight of his eighty-two plus years. His body seems simply to be collapsing. The doctor thinks he can live out the month, perhaps a bit longer. For a week or more he has rarely been fully conscious. He occasionally asks to see the bishop or . . . an old friend, but does he recognize them when they come?

Because of his paralytic side he has to be taken out of bed on an average of every half hour; you [Ev] as nurse, know what this means for those who take care of him — he being as helpless as a child. If he recovers, by a first class miracle, it will be a big disappointment for him; and if he dies it will not be a great surprise for us, for we have said the prayers for the dying three times. He has a . . . constitution which refuses to give in till the last iota of strength has been spent. . . . So you see, Ev, that our Christmas joy is somewhat dampened. However, our jubilee must be in God. Then too, death for Trappists has a different meaning than it has for people in the world. I stay our pen on this subject lest I blanket your Christmas glee by an untimely discourse on death, when behold, it is the birth that we are commemorating.

We receive our Christmas mail at noon of Christmas eve, but I started this before noon knowing that Ev would surely have a letter or something there for me. I was right. My heart-sprung thanks for letter, gift, and card. I must be brief as this page is getting short.

I have never received so many and such consoling letters, cards, and Christmas gifts as this year. The most consoling and soothing letter was from dear old Father Crowley,* three pages long. The first page is beautiful; he speaks of his own desires to be a Trappist; how wise I was in my choice; and the vanity of the present life, etc. Then he tells of many of my seminary companions: some in Rome, some in Philadelphia, and some professors at St. Thomas College, St. Paul.

I may write you again if Reverend Father's death should occur, and if so I will enclose some Christmas letters — haven't read them all yet. I hasten to send this before mail time.

Have you gained the jubilee indulgence? Ask your pastor for the conditions. I would have gained one for you, but an indulgence cannot be applied to another living person.

Most earnestly will I pray for Joe's pecuniary success; tell him to place an unswerving trust in God. My whole heart's love.

fr. M. Gerard

After Dom Edmond's death, the monks elected Dom Mary Frederic Dunne to succeed him as abbot. As former prior of the community he was well known and loved by the monks. They knew that his first interest would be the spiritual welfare of the community.

One of the first acts of the newly-elected abbot was to arrange for the ordination of Frater Gerard, who became a deacon on April 6 and a priest on December 21, 1935.

Gerard's brothers and sisters, together with a number of relatives and friends, met outside the abbey church door at Gethsemani at five a.m., on his ordination day. From the gallery they

* First rector of Nazareth Hill, St. Paul, Minnesota.

easily identified the tall, thin candidate for Orders. His sole companion was a short monk from the Isle of Malta. The cold church did not disturb the visitors that day, although they wondered how the monks could survive Kentucky winters without heat in the buildings.

After the ordination, Father Gerard lost no time in coming to the guesthouse to meet the family and relatives. The joy of the day could scarcely be matched by any other earthly celebration. Abbot Frederic's face was bright with happiness as he moved from one guest to another that afternoon. He was grateful because God had blessed the young monk and brought him through his passover into the promised land of the priesthood.

The newly ordained priest offered Mass the next morning in the visitors' chapel, where the relatives gathered to offer with him the great sacrifice of thanksgiving.

The following letters are typical of the young monk's gratitude.

Christmas Day 1935

Dear Eva and Joe:

The last four or five days seem as a dream from which I have not yet fully recovered. This is the first letter I pen with my consecrated hands — those hands over which the holy oils flowed and over which the Bishop prayed, "Whatever they bless it shall be blessed, and whatever they consecrate it shall be consecrated." Surely, "God has chosen the weak things of this world and those things which are naught to perform His greatest works." The awful power, too, of celebrating Holy Mass, of forgiving sins are above all the deserts and merits of even the angels, and yet, God, whose ways are inscrutable, has chosen the last and the least of our family to fulfill those holy functions. May He be forever blessed for His infinite mercy and love, and may He take me out of this world rather than allow me ever to willingly offend Him.

This Christmas was one of overwhelming gifts and graces, but my poor heart has been sorely sore even amidst all the splendor and brightness around. If I experience a heartache when the visit of only one is over, well, you can suppose what it was when all my earthly dear ones so suddenly appear and depart again. In a day or two I will again be serene and happy at heart.

I offered three Holy Masses this morning; one was for all those I love, living and dead. Reverend Father gave us priests one Mass for our own intention. I confess a little tear trickled down as I went on with that last Mass.

I can in no wise express how pleased I was and how I appreciated your coming on that day, which, as I said, now seems as a day about which one dreams. The sacrifices, too, which so many made in order to be present! May our dear Lord, who alone knows how to reward loving acts, requite their marks of affection with His own reward one day. I know most of it was prepared by you and Sister Myron. The many letters from so many whom I had nearly forgotten, but still love, were Sister Myron's work, I know. Many were so touching. . . .

May the dear little Savior overwhelm you with His heavenly kisses.

fr. M. Gerard

Our Lady of the Gethsemani
June 16, 1936

My dear Sister [Ev]:

I thought of sending a card this time, but if we make this about card length, it will do as well.

I am earnestly hoping that your exams* were a success. Many a prayer has been said for that intention. Of course, God's ways are not our ways and often He, as a good Father, must refuse us one petition to give us something better; this is the teaching of St. Augustine.

When I first read your letter, I read July 3 for June 3, so your Mass was said on the feast of Corpus Christi, June 9th, surely a beautiful day. There is no past or future with God; all is present. Then, too, the Blessed Virgin was preserved from original sin in view of the future merits of Jesus; so I am sure that the Holy Mass and my other prayers were *on time* for your request, if it really be for your true good.

---

* Ev was in college at this time.

Our temperature has been hovering around 90 to 95 degrees, but for a week or more a steady northern breeze has driven it down considerably. We have very little hope, however, that it is going to stay there. Our June, July, and August have entered into an allied contract — nothing under 90 degrees — rarely do they perjure themselves. . . .

Thanks much for your kind offer, but I know of nothing right now. We are much in need of rain and all of Kentucky with us. God sends His rain on the good and the wicked; so we can still hope, for His eternal mercy does not change. Next Friday is the feast of the Sacred Heart; may its light and love be poured upon you. As life wastes and fades away, it is so consoling to have this Heart on which to lean the whole weight of our eternal well-being.

O Sacred Heart, keep us,
fr. M. Gerard

Many of Gerard's letters were addressed to the brothers and sisters collectively and sent to different individuals, depending upon the contents of the letter, or just for the sake of variety. The letters were forwarded by the different individual family members to one another. The letters from the family to Father Gerard were often in the form of a round robin.

Trappist, Kentucky
Dec. 25, 1936

My very dear Brothers and Sisters:

From pole to pole there is music in the air, and love and joy seem to have broken loose and are running wild in every heart and on every tongue. It is amid the soul-soothing and heart-ravishing glamour of it all that I, too, come in turn to wish you all a most Merry Christmas, a season filled with such joy and peace as will rejuvenate your souls despite worldly cares and will one day bloom into sheaves of heavenly bliss and glory. And may the New Year be an echo and a continuation of the same gifts and prosperity.

Well, it is Christmas afternoon so we will just sit down and in the sight of the "Three of the Crib" have a little fireside talk about old things and new. We'll even allow Bill to smoke one of his good hand-rolled cigars, if he derives any solace therefrom. I rather think that the consolation of most smokers is in the pipe itself, for we are all sort of "kids" of an older growth, you know, and we need something to play with.

To me Christmas is closely intertwined with Johnny's and Raphael's* many, many-toned "Merry Christmas." . . . [Then] everything seemed to be flush and laved all over with delight and charm, and my whole being seemed to be canopied with the glory of heaven. Santa Claus never had much part in my young life; when my turn came, Father and Mother had just about tired of playing their false role. So I had very few delights from those weird chimney visits, except on those disillusioning occasions when Syl would persist in replacing some of my time-worn [stuffed] cats and tops in my nightly-hung stocking. The fervid glisten in my eyes would suddenly fade when I discovered the old, rent cat and lopsided top. For me Santa Claus was metamorphosed into a Miss Santa Claus in the person of Ag. How I used to admire her, endowed, as I believed, with some preternatural powers of calling forth ready-made gifts from the Christmas tree. It was her duty to read off the names. The Christmases at home were not so delightful; because of running errands hither and thither my longing eye was too often drawn from the soliciting, gift-laden tree. What I say of myself was, I suppose, more or less the experience of all. . . . We spent two or three Christmases at Bill's, but I don't believe we were ever all present; especially Mother's absence caused a joy-dampening void. And now I suppose our next family Christmas will take place in the eternal years in our unchangeable home.

I hope you all spent a good Christmas in the spiritual order first, and were not excluded from a good white-breasted turkey dinner, the kind Syl likes.

Ev was telling me how Joe complained one day after dinner

* Johnny and Raphael Farrell, relatives.

that his good appetite is falling off something "awful." Ev explained how on that particular occasion he had only been able to relish two-thirds of the turkey. I hope your appetites are falling off in that same direction. . . .

Good old Father Crowley, Rector of Nazareth Hall, wrote a beautiful letter enclosing pictures of Nazareth Hall and of Archbishop Dowling's funeral. . . .

On Christmas morning Reverend Father* allowed us all to say one Mass for our own intention. So you can all say that you have a Christmas Mass in your spiritual coffers, and if I possessed all the wealth in the U.S.A., I couldn't offer you a gift more precious. (P.S. The sight of the chalice you all gave me kept you in mind.)

For the rest, my dear sisters and brothers, let us try to love God and love one another, for this was the repeated and whole burden of St. John's sermons, the Apostle of love, on whose feast day I am finishing this.

May the divine Babe of the Crib press you to His heart and weld your wills to His in a union of mutual, sacrificing, and genuine love. Please ask this grace for me.

Your little brother,
fr. M. Gerard

The newly ordained priest desired to make love his great aim in life. "Love inclines one to find happiness in the happiness of the beloved," *he wrote to his brothers and sisters.* "Love depersonalizes as one goes out to another. Therefore, to make Jesus happy, to please Him, must be our sole aim. We must be lovers, for is it reasonable to expect a warm embrace from our Father at the end of our life if we have not loved Him in time? Love, in clear terms, means doing God's will."

On All Saints' Day, 1937, Father Gerard wrote an encouraging letter to those at home.

* Abbot Frederic Dunne.

Trappist, Ky.
Nov. 1, 1937.

My dear Brothers and Sisters All:

Happy feast day. Today the Church invites us to take a look toward heaven. And wonders indeed arrest our eye. There we see souls who have walked this earth clothed with humanity, and who have experienced all the feelings of pleasure and disgust, weariness, and likes and dislikes which beset us; souls of once young men and women, who in the very bloom of youth when all the world seemed one long rapturous song of pleasure and delight; when all its path seemed beauty-strewn, even the color added, but often alas — shimmering falsely. At that very hour, the golden dawn of life, they turned from all its dazzling panorama and looked down another avenue — the way which Jesus trod. They beheld His divinely beauteous features worn and haggard from suffering; they looked into His blood-shot eyes which whispered love to their hearts, not earthly love but love eternal. Jesus, the very thought of Him, with sweetness filled their hearts; Jesus, the divine lover of souls, the stealer of hearts. They saw He was quite alone, bearing a cross and weighed down with the reproaches of men — the divine outcast.

A vision of the world's gayety loomed up on one side: the thoughtless merriment of the dance-hall, the thrill of the theater, the sweetness of close friendship, travels and excursions with their varied and awe-inspiring scenery, all this and more, flowered and perfumed with, perhaps, lofty imaginative powers, seethed over their minds and tugged at their hearts. . . . Then, perhaps some staunch and thundering truism, as: "What doth it profit a man, if he gain the whole world and suffer the loss of his immortal soul?" beat in upon them. . . . They balanced the years of time and eternity; with Gospel in hand viewed again the joys and pains of life, and an eternity of happiness in contrast to one of woe.

For many of them, perhaps for all, it was the zero hour of their lives, their eternal loss or gain. With a stout resolve, courage and heroism greater than any ever displayed on a battle-field of war, they turned and, meeting the questioning eye of Jesus, joined hands with the man of sorrows, with Him whose look was hidden and despised. They stopped on the way of the cross, the ascent up Calvary. They were not alone; no, they were leaning on their Beloved. They were not trusting in themselves; they were aided by the arm of an almighty God. Thenceforth for them life indeed had another meaning; time was but a passage to eternity. All their mundane fairy-dreams had coalesced into the Sacred Heart of Jesus. All their loves of earth had amalgamated into the bosom of love eternal. Their lives merged into the life of Jesus — a life devoted to the divine will.

They loved and hated what Jesus loved and hated; they began to do God's holy will on earth as they are now doing it in heaven, where their jubilee is in God. These, then, are the saints who dwelt amongst us and whose feast we are celebrating today. They are gathered from every avocation of life. Some were thought to be saints while still on earth; others were considered somewhat below the average in their state of life. Some for a time were enmeshed in the thralldom of sin; others never sullied their baptismal robe. There are those who passed their lives on the pinnacles of the world, while others passed their lives in the wilderness of obscurity. On the brows of a few the Church has canonically placed the aureola of certain sanctity, but the vast majority are counted among the general multitude, who stand before the throne of God and of the Lamb, the elect of all nations and peoples and tongues. They wait our arrival and long to exclaim our final victory over the world, the flesh, and the devil. Will the sequel of our lives be glorious? Yes, if we follow the saints, or rather, follow Him whom they followed. I better stop here abruptly lest another page or two glide by under my pen.

We had two solemn professions today: one young man from Mexico, another from St. Louis. It is an event of joy, but not unmixed with tears, especially as the father and mother of the St. Louis boy were both present. They will soon become inured to separation as they now have a daughter, a Carmelite, and a Trappist son. I noticed four nuns in the group, but I cannot believe his Carmelite sister was among them.

Reverend Father returned from Europe and told us of his experience by land and sea. His chief sea story was "sickness"; he ate once on ship.

One of our monasteries celebrated the eighth centenary of its foundation. The bishop of the diocese held a diocesan synod on the grounds of the monastery as a part of the celebration. The object of it was to increase devotion to Mary the Mother of God in individual homes. The Holy Father sent a cardinal *a latere.* The first day was for the young women — fifteen thousand were present. Mass in the open air; it rained heavily, but not one moved. The second day was for women — fifty thousand were present. The third day was for men — over one hundred thousand were present. A diocesan synod!

Reverend Father went to Rome, saw the Holy Father, visited the chief churches and shrines. He was down in the catacombs, etc. He went to Lisieux and was with the three sisters of the Little Flower for a couple of hours. He said Mass in the death chamber of St. Thérèse; everything is left just as it was when she died. Sister Marie, the oldest, is quite infirm. Reverend Father said he had to give her Communion in the wheel chair aside from the others. All are aging; Celine, I guess, still preserves the high spirits. The crypt of the basilica is finished — the zenith of beauty. Bill and Syl helped to pay for it. I wish I could show you the picture of it which Reverend Father brought home. Mother Agnes hopes it will be finished in three years. They had a National Eucharistic Congress at Lisieux last summer.

I am finishing this on All Souls' Day. Priests may say three Masses today. You all shared in each. We sang the Office of the Dead, all of it, Vespers, Lauds, and Nocturns . . . a pontifical High Mass, followed by a procession through chapter, cemetery, and cloisters; then the penitential psalms.

Right now we are husking corn, so fast, in fact, that the brothers cannot haul it in rapidly enough. Our corn was not extraordinarily good, but better than that grown on Wisconsin soil. I do not wish to disparage Wisconsin, not only because Bill and Veronica* are still noble dwellers within its confines, but especially because it is truly a "superior" state.

May Jesus with all His saints bless you.
fr. M. Gerard

---

* William's wife.

One of the duties of a priest is to preach. Father Gerard told his Benedictine sister, "I fear I share the plight of the archbishop of St. Paul, who said that he lost both sleep and appetite when, as a young curate, his pastor told him that he was to preach the next Sunday. He feared that the whole pulpit was going to cave in."

In his letters, Father Gerard gave his brothers and sisters short summaries of his sermons, and described his relief after completing a particularly difficult assignment. After giving a sermon on St. John's day, 1937, he wrote to Sister Myron:

Deo gratias et Mariae—it's over. I feel a hundred pounds lighter in the head and heart. Our dear Lord saved me the humiliation of having to stop and take a seat right in the middle of it. When I become as holy as the Cure d' Ars, He may judge me strong enough to bear such things *suaviter et fortiter*. You know the good Cure did not get by very big in many of his sermons. His first failed as flat as a pancake.

Well, Sister, I know how dear St. John is to you, and therefore it is that I am writing to you. This is the first Christmas word I have penned. And really in writing this I am stealing time, for I have some heavy exams December 30. You know *neo-sacerdotes* must keep up their studies and exams for some years after ordination. I have Moral Theology this time. You may say I am not stealing much time, for this looks more like a racetrack than a dignified letter. . . .

Oh, Christmas, what a beautiful time it is! Here this year, I never saw such a magnificent Christmas panorama. On Christmas eve when we arose, every branch, bush, and twig had on a two-inch fleecy frosting. Every cedar on the knolls was gracefully bowing under the weight of the snow. Eight inches . . . had fallen during the night, and what monstrous flakes! Yet during it all there was not a sound to break the perfect and sweet silence of the Christmas night. Were I a poet . . . I might pause here to give a more comprehensive picture of it all. . . .

My third Mass on Christmas was for my own intentions . . . be assured that you had a big memento, too. . . . I had to time the first Mass so that the community could sing the *sub tuum* at the beginning of the second, and this gave me an especially long time, as they were meditating. . . .

Dear Sister Myron, I hope the Holy Infant brought you loads of good health all laved over with His spiritual gifts of His love. Pray for me; I do for you. Greet all, and the choicest blessings for the New Year.

fr. M. Gerard

The Trappist wanted to spread the Good News to the family by encouraging them to study the Scriptures and the liturgy.

Jan. 1, 1938

My dear Sisters:

. . . You may wonder who the addressees are meant to be . . . Sister Myron and sister Agnes. As I had permission, I thought I'd write a little letter to each this Christmas rather than my usual family letter. Still you two have so much in common that I deemed it all right to unite you again in this letter. What are your special bonds? You live in the same state, both under the special protection of a saint — St. Joseph and St. Paul.

Sister Myron, it is only now that Ag is starting to study the Bible. That is only one of the advantages of a St. Paul resident.* She will enjoy the Psalms, and some of those beautiful books: Job, Judith, Books of Wisdom. From so many quarters I have received news that the laity are taking on a new impetus in the cause of religion. Syl spoke of it. Father Crowley mentioned it. I enjoy dear old Father Crowley's letter each year; he is so cordial and so priestly. He was the first rector of Nazareth. He is now pastor of Holy Name Parish, Minneapolis.

I suppose, Sister Myron, that the Christmas season is a rather busy one for you. Sister Claire said she saw little of you. She added: "We might just as well be Trappists." At first I thought you must be enjoying a delightful solitude — St. Bernard's "O *beata solitudo, O sola beatitudo.*" . . .

Feast days in a convent especially in the motherhouse are so heavenly, with little of earth's evaporating joys.

* Ed and Agnes had recently left the farm and moved to St. Paul.

I like to occupy the days immediately surrounding Christmas in the study of the Liturgy and in quiet contemplation of the season's beautiful feasts and mysteries. Of course, when the will of God directs otherwise, we must then partake of that other spiritual life, which although less sweet, is not less meritorious; in fact, is more meritorious just because it is less sweet. It is a life filled with God's good pleasure, the simple *fiat* of abandonment to His holy ways.

I know not, Sister Myron, if you have anything to do with the books of the community, but we have now a beautiful book for reading before Compline: *Abandonment to Divine Providence* by Rev. J. P. DeCaussade, S.J., translated from the complete French edition by E. J. Strickland. It contains not only the theoretical part but also "Letters of Direction." . . . I recommend it highly as a superb ascetical work. . . .

Again, God keep you and bless you during the ensuing year.

Yours in Jesus,
fr. M. Gerard

April 17, 1938

My dear Brothers and Sisters:

It is Easter morning, and doubtless your souls are filled with joy and gratitude to our dearest Lord for all He has done for us. . . . As we followed Him through the dolors of the past week, we must have been ever more and more impressed with the thought that God surely has loved the world, and so loved it as to give His only Son to save that world, to recall it to Himself. Jesus has given us an example, an example of self-sacrifice, of a will clinging unflinchingly to the will of God, to His good pleasure.

Does the world appreciate and requite His love? Yes, many; for Jesus will be loved and praised unto the end. Many stand by with folded arms, unmoved by staring facts and unquestionable evidence, and, as it were uninterested in all that passes about them — out of joint with the times. There are those, too, who are armed against God and against His Christ, seemingly hating Him the more furiously just because of His love. . . .

In another sense, we ought not to be surprised at those things at all, for a vein of God-hating runs through the whole history of the human race from the first sin of Adam. Jesus said to His hearers: "You have both hated Me and hated Him who sent Me." "In the world you shall have persecution. If they have hated Me, they will hate you also." In the end they will all be forced to exclaim with Julian the Emperor: "Nazarene, Thou hast conquered." But alas, it was not a cry of love.

When one steps back, viewing things as a bystander, and sees time speeding on with rapid pace, and compares this short span of life on earth with the eternal years, with endless life, the more and more persuaded one becomes that if there be one sane thing to do in this world it is to "stick" to God, to cling to Jesus through thick or thin, through likes and dislikes, through light or darkness. God has spoken; He has revealed Himself and His holy will; His words are true. Why, the very essence of truth must be sought in God. For anything is true only in so far as it is conformed to the divine mind, in so far as it is that which God wills it to be.

The liturgy during those Lenten days was so full of consoling instruction. I have in mind especially the Gospels of the Mass; among others, the condition after death of the rich man and that of poor Lazarus who begged crumbs from the rich man's table. Lazarus in heaven and the rich man in hell (not because he was rich simply, but because he used his riches for self-gratification instead of being helpful and charitable to his neighbor) calling to Lazarus to wet his finger in water and come to ease his burning tongue. His request was refused, for he had deliberately chosen hell for himself. When Dives asked at least to send someone from the dead to warn his family lest they also perish, again, no. They have the Scriptures; if they don't pay attention to them, an apparition of the dead would soon be put out of mind, too. And how true. . . . No one can be pushed into heaven against his will. As the poet says, "We are captains of our souls." Judas had grace to be saved just as well as had St. Peter. Both had sinned, both had denied Jesus. St. Bernard says St. Peter was the greater sinner of the two. Both acknowledged their sin and repented bitterly, St. Peter in tears of confidence and love; Judas in tears of despair, mistrusting the infinite and never-refused mercy and goodness of Jesus.

Oh, let us never mistrust Jesus; for nothing so wounds Him as lack of confidence, and nothing so honors Him as perfect trust in His love and mercy.

Retracing our steps, this is Easter, and I wish you all the joys and fairest graces of the day. I congratulate you on the very good Lent you have spent. One mentioned it was the best yet. Each Lent is drawing us nearer and nearer to that last Lent that will be our final preparation for our last Easter on earth when our bodies rise glorious — oh, good Jesus, grant — from the tomb.

The other day I was adding up how many more years I might count on. I have been wearing the holy habit twelve years this Easter. Is that not about one third of my time, at least a fourth? My final conclusion was, "What matters it? Be ready for one or for fifty years." The big thing in every state or condition of life is to be man enough and saint enough to accept what God wills and appoints. And if at any time we don't find that disposition solidly established within us, let us get down on our knees before the altar or the crucifix until it be given us, for it is a necessary grace, and therefore it will never be refused us.

I am glad you have been as well as can be expected. I, too, have avoided any serious illness, barring the fact that my bony structure is somewhat in evidence, in such wise that right now I look even more like a scarecrow than I usually do. This is the first year since I came to Gethsemani that we have not had the flu.

Reverend Father is in Providence, R. I. He will return in two weeks.

Everything is green and growing here. The temperature is perfect — 75°. We have had an abundance of rain this spring. Our water dam, not being completed, retains none of it. We will be thirsty next summer. . . .

Again, may this Eastertide be a sunny one for you all, and know no vesper hour.

Your brother in Jesus and Mary,
fr. M. Gerard

Father Gerard gave retreats to priests and laymen for a number of years. He felt keenly the need of grace to help him with his work. Often he asked a former teacher, Sister Elaine, for prayers. He wrote, "If Jesus does not live in me, what good will I do to the old pastors and monsignori twice my age? . . . So much good is done, Sister, by these retreats. [The retreatants] come in groups of fifty and sixty: lawyers, doctors, farmers, and all. Some have been out of the church for forty years."

Once he remarked, "We have over forty priests here on retreat this week. They are very silent and quiet — their bishop is with them."

Though his life took on a rather serious cast in the monastery while giving retreats, he did not lose his characteristic sense of humor.

May 28, 1938

My dear Sister Myron:

Tell your good Sister Jeroma, or I should say, your Benedictine Sister Jeroma, that your Trappist brother received her Mass stipend, and Mass will be said for all her intentions.

I am continuing this on Ascension Thursday. Our morning was occupied with Office, chapter, and pontifical ceremonies. I suppose there were fifty sisters here for pontifical Mass today. I hope they went away in the same good sentiments with which the apostles returned to Jerusalem after Jesus had ascended.

We have Dom Celsus, Abbot of Mt. Melleray, Ireland, here. He has a daughterhouse in Iowa which he is officially visiting. He told us how the Irish got the Communists out of Ireland — a very Irish way. They hired a man famous for throwing bottles to assist at the first great meeting. He greeted the speaker by shaving off a few hairs of his head with a bottle. As the speaker went on undaunted, he threw another that grazed his cheek. They [the Irish] haven't been troubled with Communists since.

You ask of my well-being. Last November I had a little fever that brought me down, and I've been pretty well down ever since. . . . No T.B. germs, so I suppose there is not much danger for fifty years or so more.

Our weather this May has been rather warm — what will the summer be? Our crops look good; our wheat will be turning ripe in a week or two. We generally harvest under a 130° sun. . . .

I hope the Holy Ghost will fill your soul with all His gifts, through the intercession of the Queen of Heaven and Earth, in whom I am

fr. M. Gerard

June 8, 1939

Dear Eve and Joe:

This is *Corpus Christi*, the feast of the Blessed Sacrament, our greatest earthly consolation — really our heaven upon earth, enjoyed, however, in faith and amid suffering. Interior and exterior suffering is man's way on earth. . . .

What pitiful pleas for prayer we get at times. I sometimes ease my feelings by the thought that the reality cannot be quite as desperate as the pen-picture. Still, God help poor suffering humanity. Those in sin, however, are to be compassionated above and beyond all others. . . . What must it be for a soul to fall into hell? "Broad is the way, and many there are who enter in thereat" — an awful thought. Dante gives a most graphic conception of hell. What would one not do to rescue those blind, unthinking passion-guided souls. Suffering and prayer become almost a pleasure when one realizes that by uniting them to the sufferings and merits of Jesus, they are the most powerful means we have for the salvation of souls. I don't suppose with all your work you have got to Dante yet, but you may someday. . . .

In Corde Jesu,
fr. M. Gerard

August 19, 1939

My dear Sister Elaine,

Perhaps I would not have received permission to write to little Sister Elaine simply, but I easily obtained permission to write to sick Sister Elaine. Our Lord said that He is going to grant heaven to those who visit the sick; and St. Benedict, you know, exhorts us to exercise all solicitude towards the infirm.

And so, Sister, because of the divine behests and the allowances of the Holy Rule, I am most happy to take up our somewhat unexercised pen, hoping that these few words written and read *propter Jesum* will alleviate for a moment your sickroom ennui and bring your memories joyfully back to childhood. . . .

Time goes fast, Sister, whenever one is regulated by bells. I might whisper: we have more bells in the monastery than you have. One just sounded vesper hour.

August twentieth is the feast of St. Bernard, the glory of our Order and of the whole Church. Blessed Gerard was his brother. Read St. Bernard's twenty-sixth sermon on the Canticle of Canticles.

Did Sister Myron get you reading Dante? You gave me the *Inferno* years ago. You can suppose how I appreciated him in first year high. I am reading him now with relish. I read *New Life* and just passed out of hell the other day. Awful, isn't it? Yet [Dante] is very dogmatic and sound.

Well, Sister, as time is rushing on and you are even now in the hospital, and I am no longer a Samson either, let's make a compact. The one who gets to heaven first will never cease praying for the other. O.K.?

I am shelving things together, for I must stop with this page. . . . You may be sure of a memento at Holy Mass, and don't forget me at Communion.

In Mary and her St. Bernard,
fr. M. Gerard

On the 4th of July, 1939, Father Gerard received a letter from his Sister in religion, to which he replied:

"I was pleased to get your letter. It was sort of a 4th of July firecracker. St. Benedict does not favor the other kind which disturbs silence. Even our neighbors seem to sense that, for I haven't heard a shot on the 4th since I've been in the monastery. However, it is just possible that purchase money was lacking. . . ."

The young monk liked to invite his family and close friends to join him in projects from time to time. His letters at this time reflected special interest in the study of Dante and St. Thomas.

August 20, 1939

My dear Brothers and Sisters:

The feast of St. Bernard, the glory of our Order, the light and man of his century. Perhaps, too, one of the greatest saints in heaven. It is a first-class feast with us. The bells ring joyfully, the organ chimes . . . and decorations abound; in fine, as an Italian would say, all the psalms end in *Gloria*.

The second paragraph of our summer letters generally begin by vituperating Kentucky and its heat. This year, however, we have gotten rain in due season. It rained this morning — and excepting two or three sharp cuts in June and July, we had a very tolerable summer, thanks not to the mythical weatherman, but to the Governor of the weather, the good Lord Himself. . . .

Our novitiate is rather large now, thanks to the Inspirer of all good. The last time I counted we had thirty-six novices. If the good Lord continues to send us vocations, we will soon have to found a new monastery — in Wisconsin or in Minnesota, where milk and honey flow in abundance; where the world's best water bubbles and gushes forth, and where the . . . temperature renews the youth of its joyful inhabitants. O blessed land which has been so laved all over with heaven's benedictions and which nestles so gracefully in the full sheen of a special protecting Providence. The very memory . . . evokes sweet reveries which well up and linger in one's heart. . . .

As I said, we have lots of rain, and the crops look good. The corn is many feet tall, too tall for a common man to pick the ears. Most years we can cut it with a good "Bluegrass" corn knife, but this year we'll have to lay an ax to its roots, I guess. We have peaches this year . . . juicy ones, too. The garden, too, seems to yield its fruits in due measure. I must confess that I haven't set foot in its precincts this year.

I have not heard much about Dante from any of you. I presume you are all reading the Gospels — the best life of Christ we have.

I just got out of Dante's hell — an awful place. I read *Vita Nova*, too. . . .

Dante is very theological and very scriptural in his conceptions, if indeed he had not a real vision. Too, his views accord very well with most private revelations. I know not if I ever told you of the rather weird old woman I met in Milwaukee. She had visions of hell occasionally, and what she told me of things down there squares perfectly with Dante's exposition. Some theologians were of the opinion that hell is in the center of the earth, and Dante says it is there he found Satan.

However, it is a general truism that one will break with sin and advance in divine love far more rapidly by meditating on heaven and its inhabitants, Jesus, Mary, and the saints, than by considering the devil and his horde. Still the dread of hell fire is not to be put aside wholly, for it is only fear that will keep some souls out of the meshes of sin. If there be any fool under the sun, it is he who wallows in sin. And yet, considering our own perverse inclinations, how easily we err in judgment; how our will adheres to evil. We can only compassionate the wayward and pray God on our knees that He preserve our own souls in the right way, or bring us back to the arms of His love if we have followed our lower nature rather than right reason or that which is the same, conscience. For conscience is the intellect itself in as much as it judges concerning the righteousness or deformity of an act to be placed here and now. Sin, it is true, resides in the will, but there is nothing in the will which was not first pondered in the mind. The will, being a blind faculty, needs the illuminative rays and instruction of the intellect. The will, however, can direct this light along proper channels, down the lines of right thought. We are then, in common parlance, "thinking straight." The will, too, can turn the mind away from the consideration of truth; this leaves one in vincible ignorance, voluntary ignorance, tantamount to a state of sin.

Again, the will may adhere to falsehood, embrace what it sees is not true. Sin is manifested here. The intellect may not get things straight and thus proposes to the will evil for real good. This is invincible ignorance and no sin, supposing sufficient diligence was used in the search, consideration, and study of things.

Well, by filling the mind with truth and the will with a big love for the good, the true, and the beautiful, we will step clear of all those stumbling blocks which strew the way of our salvation.

How did we get going down those avenues of thought? Dante, I guess, gave us a bad steer a couple of pages back. . . . Sister Myron is reading Dante, as you perhaps know.

My health is very good. Of course, I still have to eat butter instead of jelly and beans instead of candy. . . .

May our dear Lord and His Blessed Mother keep you all in good health and so guide our lives that we may be together one day in heaven.

fr. M. Gerard

Nov. 1, 1939

My dear Brothers and Sisters All:

We are celebrating the feast of All Saints — of many near and dear to us whom we have known, walked and conversed with in life. Mother and Father, I hope, are already there; however, they will continue to have a memento at Mass.

The feast of All Saints! Who were the saints? They were men and women of love. What made them saints? Love, the obedience of charity.

Love is a word so misused and misapplied that when we speak of real love, we must denominate it charity. Love is often used to denote inclinations, sentimentalism, natural instincts. This is a besmirching of that noble sentiment implied by the word love.

According to St. Thomas, to love is to aspire to unite oneself with the object loved; it is a movement towards good in order to possess it. The truer and higher this good is, the nobler is the aspiring love. Bossuet says, "The character of love is to tend to the closest and most intimate union that can exist — the union of two wills." So love, then, is a sovereign power, a superior force which draws us out of ourselves to unite us to another.

If the object of our love be a natural good — creatures — and have no higher aim or motive, well, it begins and ends in time. It will have no place in eternity, for it was in no wise referred to God. And what is not God, neither from nor for God, cannot be eternal.

Is, then, the love of creatures and creation a waste of time? Yes, if God be in everywise excluded, viewing things as a Christian should *in specie aeternitatis*, in lasting values. But to love creatures and creation as being God's handiwork, to love the good, the true, the beautiful as seen in creatures because they were planted there by God and are bits reflecting His divine perfections, is not only mind-elevating but soul-sanctifying as well; and what is more, it is going to enter into and form part of our eternal, unending joy. Therefore it is that St. Thomas (I always feel in good company when quoting him) says that God is to be loved for His own sake and our neighbor not for his own sake — which is sometimes impossible — but for God's sake, because he is a child of God, because God loves him. "He loves all He has made"; because, finally, God commands this love.

To love one's fellowman for his own sake, because of the good we perceive in him as of himself is naturally noble, but it is simple philanthropy. It lives and dies in time; since it is not supernatural it has no value with God. It cannot attain an eternal reward.

Could we but look out upon the earth with an all-seeing eye, we would doubtless be overawed by the woeful waste that goes on daily. Grand efforts and high achievements, aiming low, ending in the sod, which, had they but a bit higher impetus, had the intention been tinged with the supernatural, might have gleaned lofty and lasting recognitions and rewards. Here we are running right into the secret of the saints. They are saints because they supernaturalized their lives; they divinized their love. They knew they had a head and a heart, and they used them. They motivated their acts, thus making them human acts and not merely acts of a man.

They were true philosophers in practice if not also in theory, for they went to the last causes of things. No effect without a cause. Things exist. Who is the cause? Intelligent effects mean an intelligent cause — a being a se, God. Has He spoken? What is His will? Finally, through a straight line of reasoning, they came right down to the truth that the Savior who has come, Jesus, has put into our hands the means to turn everything into supernatural love and values, through His own merits.

Love breathes and inspires confidence. Power and love are the foundations of every act of confidence. Confidence, placed in or born even of creatures, has a nerving and joy-giving effect. It spurs one on to higher and nobler endeavor. What then will the knowledge and pondered truth that an all-powerful and all-good Father loves me, do for my soul? Why, it will simply metamorphose my life and affections; it will cause to well up and burn within me sweet and soothing fires, fires of jubilant and never-ending hopes.

To learn divine things from human: how eager earthly lovers are to hear and read each other's words. Thus, the soul that has come to the realization of God's love for her will earnestly seek out what God has said; to hear more of His whisperings of love, and to learn what He asks of her to prove her affection for Him. Since He loves her and she loves Him, the soul wishes to be united to Him — to do His holy will, knowing that the closest union of love is the union of wills. And in this very union of wills is contained the sum total of all perfection. So in this devotion to God's holy will lies the sanctity of the saints whose feast we are celebrating today. And it is the same supernaturalizing of our lives by union with God's holy will that will sanctify our souls, and one day number us among the saints. That this aureola of sanctity rest upon the brow of us all is my wish on this Hallowmas eve. . . .

In the monastery all goes as usual. We are putting up a novitiate and a corn crib. The sides of the old crib are bulging out with excess of corn, and the walls of the novitiate are bulging with novices. All our crops were good.

Reverend Father did not go to general chapter this year — they had none. His health seems good; in fact, I have never seen him sick a day since I came to the monastery. . . .

A cool autumn is settling down upon us. The goblins of evenings past stripped the oaks of all their adornment, leaving them like empty choirs where once gay birds sang. The mocking bird, the dearest of them all, just yesterday hymned his sweetest yet pathetic last farewell.

I commend you all to the angels and saints, asking them to keep you under their protecting care.

In the love of Jesus and Mary,
fr. M. Gerard

When Father Gerard heard rumors that his only single brother, Syl, was to be married, he took the opportunity to write to the family on vocations, particularly about the religious life and the marriage state.

Our Lady of Gethsemani
Nov. 2, 1942

My dear Ones All:

Letters have passed and repassed since my last "round word" to you all.

In all these communications there is a shadowing or foreshadowing (for some of ye more cultured: adumbration) signifying something shaping into final form in St. Paul. Syl's name is mentioned generally in the same letter, sometimes in the same line, even as a joint compound with Madeline.* I hand this over to you G-men to weigh, measure, compare and define whether it indicates or denotes friendship or marriage. Friendship is a social generality; marriage is also cosmic.

There are many ways to love God. Two deserve mention. First, to seek the divine through the divine; this is the religious life. Second, is to seek the divine through the human and this is the marriage state.

In order to seek the divine through the divine, the religious must remove the obstacles; he must put things human out of his life; he must cut away his attachment to things of earth, to things of sense. This he does by the vow of chastity. By this vow he is able to show more reverence to God. He knows that the love of creatures is good, but the love of the Creator is supreme. He establishes in his soul God alone. This vow of a religious is not a suppression or a repression, as modern psychologists would have it, but a domination over the lower part of man in order to free the spiritual part. He puts aside the drops of love of earth in order to more perfectly attain that which is infinite, divine love. He suppresses the pleasures of the flesh for those of the spirit. The vow of chastity means the suffering of the loss of things of earth to purchase the joys of heaven.

People protest mildly in face of the religious vocation. They cannot see a young man or woman set aside the lights and the glamor of the world right in the bloom and blossom of youth to enter the shadows of the cross where saints are made. They can see a person being attracted to a passing love and beauty, but not to the eternal and to the divine.

---

* Syl's future wife.

God has a right to reach down and pluck roses of the earth for Himself and this He does when He calls a young man or woman to the religious state or to the priesthood.

It is well for fathers and mothers to know the signs in general of a religious vocation. What are they?

1. The desire for the state.
2. The aptitude or fitness to fulfill the duties thereof.

I see Bill looking at Veronica and saying: "After silver jubilee and eight children, we now find all was a mistake." Well, there is another way to love God, by seeking the divine through the human. The marriage state is a holy and divine institution. It is heresy to say that holy matrimony is an obstacle to salvation; therefore, if it is not an obstacle and because it is a Sacrament of the Church, it is positive help to the saving and sanctification of our souls.

St. Paul, in speaking of the sacraments, says, "I speak of a great sacrament." To show the perfection of this union between a married pair he gives the model of the love of Christ for the Church.

The married couple when they promise fidelity to each other for life seal this vow by their eternal salvation. For they promise God to stand by their contract; if they fail in their word they are failing in a most serious matter before God. And remember that God is not mocked.

The vow of matrimony induces a serious obligation which is not to be undertaken upon the first flare of passion. Greater emphasis must be put on love, on that permanent, peaceful heart-sprung love and less on sexual attraction.

The love of husband and wife must be eternal — "till the sands of the desert grow cold." That first and sensible love, the first effusion of affection after the marriage ceremony, the joy of the honeymoon are going to pass away. There is going to come the moment of disillusionment; the married pair are going to see each other as they are actually, no longer as they appeared in the sheen of aspiring affection, but simply as creatures, sons of Adam and Eve, filled with imperfections on the right and on the left.

At this time it is well to remember that there are no angels upon earth and that it is impossible for two creatures to get along habitually without the spirit of sacrifice. "In order to retain any joy we must be prepared to sustain the passing sorrows."

Passion will stop, but the bond of matrimony — the bond of mutual love — must continue on. The greatest aid to this continuance of mutual love is for each party to strive in season and out of season to make his companion for life happy. A good rule to follow is to be as sweet and amiable as possible to your companion for life. Never have a quarrel with your wife or husband. And don't forget the little courtesies which social beings owe each other in action, in words, and in attention. The children seeing the example of mother and father will imitate it and be full of affection for their parents — a household of sweetness.

There is no state of life upon the earth which has not its trials and its troubles; but if we accept those trials as coming to us from God and try to bear them in order to please Him, no matter what state we be in, we can and we will be living a happy life.

Generally, you know, in the law courts it is the husband who comes home five minutes late for supper or a wife who insists on hard boiled eggs who is being sued for divorce.

I believe that I have told you of the psychologist who [always sat down with] his wife . . . and wrote out their difficulties in a hundred words before declaring war. The result was always peace negotiations very soon. Remember Good Friday is always followed by Easter peace and joy.

However, if marriage is entered into in the right spirit and lived according to Christian principles it will afford mankind the maximum of happiness and real welfare. It is hard to conceive of a greater earthly happiness than that of a good Christian family. Family reunions prove that.

Again, marriage is the permanent pleasure of mutual love. Of course, [the married pair] may have their crosses . . . but they also have the affection and sympathy and mutual support which make sorrow lose its sting and joy to be intensified. God made marriage indissoluble, and it is a good thing that He did; otherwise human fickleness would disrupt the home.

Another joy of home life is the joy of children. When the rose color fades from the cheek of the bride (and no art can restore it), and when the cigar ashes on the carpet are intolerable, when the mother-in-law overstays her visit and the sister-in-law is not quite as acceptable a companion at the card table as she used to be, at this time a chill is apt to enter in. Something is necessary to rejuvenate the married couple. Nothing is so efficacious and so helps weld the union as a pair of baby arms to entwine the neck of father and mother, making them prisoners of love. Children are a solace especially as the years pile on. Of course, if God does not grant children that is another thing. All must submit to His holy will.

So then, the marriage state means first of all mutual affection and this affection is continued and made strong and increased by a family of children.

In order that a married life be truly what Christ desires it to be, it must be entered into with the proper spirit. The courtship ought to prove to the young man or woman that they are naturally companionable. For unless they be both saints, sensible affection and dramatic love pass away, if they are not, as I said, naturally companionable.

As this month is to see the last marriage in our family there is no need to speak of courtship except perhaps in view of parental advice.

A week has passed — a sort of public confession — since I began this letter. Since then it has been made known to me that the marriage in St. Paul has been promulgated, and it has therewith lost its G-men mystery.

I hope to send Syl and Madeline a little personal word so we'll shelve marriage for the moment.

Sister Myron launched a splendid drive for intellectual development and good reading tastes. *Companion to the Summa* [by Father Farrell] is A-1. The order of the reading is not as important as Sister would indicate. The publishing order was rather done for the sale of the volumes than as an indication for the reading order. So I have been told, and so it would seem from the volumes themselves. We have only three volumes yet. This is a real enlightening and truth-instilling work. In conversation, Father Farrell* does not strike one as of such gigantic

* Father Farrell had visited Gethsemani.

stature. He showed me some of his lectures — written lengthwise and crosswise. I didn't know how he could wade through them when time for the delivery arrived. He is very companionable. . . .

Brother Conrad, our procurator, died last Thursday. He ate well for dinner; in fact, better than usual. He had a joke or two for me — very cheerful. I looked in his room at two; he seemed asleep; I believe he was. At three-thirty Father Prior, his confessor, went to absolve him, and found him dead in bed. . . . "Be prepared, for you know not the day nor the hour." How true!

Our community is growing. We have nearly a hundred now. We'll have to be looking for another monastery soon. Where? I know not.

Reverend Father is well. He has recovered almost entirely from his attack last winter.

Our retreat will soon be on. Advent is not far distant. It is a preparation for Christmas, you know. The better the preparation, the greater the graces and gifts. Father Mateo told the priests if they do not prepare for Mass, they lose seventy percent of the graces. Apply this to the coming of Jesus on Christmas day. It applies to our Communions, too.

It seems so good to be united in Jesus on the First Fridays. January 1 will complete our ninth Friday. We better start the next set after Easter; however, this year Good Friday may not fall on the First Friday.

Well, my dear brothers and sisters, Christmas will be here soon to remind us how God loves us and has loved the world, this warring world. Yes, he hates nothing He has made. Let's return Him love. Its best expression is trust and confidence.

God bless you all in Jesus and Mary.

fr. M. Gerard

To Sister Elaine, O.S.B., a lifelong confidante of the family, Father Gerard wrote as to one of his own sisters. He traced an early attraction to the religious life to Sister's childlike simplicity in the classroom.

Our Lady of Gethsemani
January 1, 1943

Dear Sister Elaine,

Your good letter came just at the right time when Christmas hearth fires are most glowing.

The year is nearing, I hope not too nigh, when we'll send our last letter. I am thirty-six and that makes you plus, plus. Anyway I knew that you had finished your high school before I had begun. Then, too, you knew how to serve Mass before I had much suspicion that there was any such thing as Latin. The years travel on with such rapid strides that it would seem anything this side of thirty is old age.

I was glad that you met some of the family. No one was here last year — the war, no gas, no tires, etc.

Did you know L——, who was my pal in school? He was a Protestant and my room companion. I got him to say the rosary before we went to sleep. When he said it at home, the family used to kick him and say, "Get up, you fool." Well, he became a Catholic and converted his whole family. If we persevere in our devotion to Mary, our salvation is assured.

The retreats did occupy me, Sister, but I don't have them this year. I am very grateful for your prayers. I had the confessions of the novices last year. The appointments have not been given out yet this year — and you know how much grace is needed. It is easier to cut down weeds than it is to make a plant grow. . . .

Our Christmas was as usual, only more sweet this year than ever. There seemed a more abundant influx of love. I was impressed by the truth that God is love. He created out of love; He conserves, and concurs, and governs through love. He was perfectly happy in Himself. He needed no creature. St. Thomas said that He created out of goodness, therefore, for our happiness, and to share His own bliss. So all that is coming to me from creatures, things, and events — because it must be coming from God, the prime giver — is coming to me out of love. I am, as it were, swimming in love. The words of the liturgy flamed and fanned these divine whisperings in such wise that the night Office and midnight Mass were hours stolen from heaven.

Then, too, the *Puer natus est nobis; filius datus est nobis* is so uplifting and confidence-inspiring. If Jesus is mine, then the world, the nations, the saints, sinners, Mary, and God Himself, are mine, because Jesus is in all for me. Glorious, when we work that out into corollaries.

Again, I understand what it means to be a victim of love as never before. God has pent up love, and He wishes to pour it out. Therefore to be a victim of love, it suffices to accept God in all His ways; no resistance to things as they come my way. A will to please Him in everything suffices. All for Jesus, and all from Jesus. I like that because it contains the "whole law and prophets."

Well, Sister, let's again renew our compact, that we might get there. What we need is union of wills, quiet acceptance, a merging into His outlooks and loves.

God bless you the whole year through, dear Sister.

In Jesus and Mary
fr. M. Gerard

Our Lady of Gethsemani
January 3, 1944

Dear Sister Elaine,

My first word of the New Year is to you. This I suppose is in anticipation of the golden jubilee of your birth. I really thought that you were older. When at Altoona I thought you were in your thirties. I always regarded you as one of those elderly, serene and dignified nuns sitting enviously solitary amidst their spiritual lore. You were an inspiration to me, Sister — more than you supposed. Perhaps my own vocation budded and bloomed under the sheen of your charming ways and childlike sanctity. Your blithesome sweetness has often come back to me as a loving and cheering memory, and too, as a norm for a religious character. I will not say more, but I believe I could, as fifty-year-old Sisters know not the surges of self-complacency.

As you remark, your contact with children has clothed your soul with the most desirable of qualities — spiritual childhood. I will look for you with and amongst the children in heaven. Pray that I might attain those needed qualities that I might not feel too out of joint when I come to visit you in your kindergarten there.

Reverend Father called on me to give a little fervorino at a solemn profession on New Year's Day. I summarized spiritual childhood as abandon and trust, or to please Jesus and to trust Him. If I can copy the sermonette, I will send it on to you with the request that you send it on to Sister Myron for her veto or *placet*.

My patron saint is Blessed Gerard, the brother of St. Bernard. . . .

Our family is well, but we are growing old. Bill is now fifty. I say Mass for the family every first Friday, and they receive Holy Communion on that day for a happy death for all of us.

We are planning a family reunion next year here in Kentucky, of course. I will be ten years ordained then; I am getting old, too, Sister. Thirty-seven!

When fearing [death] because of God's power and majesty, why not soothe your soul with a thought of His merciful love? Be like the Little Flower. In thunder and lightning, she rejoiced and felt so confident, for God seemed close.

The fear that you experience, Sister, is, I feel, more physical than soul-sprung. The parting of body and soul, the transition into the unknown, is fear-gripping to nature. That is why I like to insist as much as possible upon clinging to the humanity of Jesus. The thought of His love-throbbing heart, the scenes of goodness and mercy of the Gospels, make Him so approachable, and His presence in me and my incorporation in Him buoy us up and allure us to Him so powerfully that we become one with Him. Then I take on His views and His loves. I then contemplate all God's attributes through the medium, the prism, of Jesus, merciful love made flesh.

Then when His power and majesty awe you, remember Jesus is this great God. He loves me. If God didn't love sinners, He would not have come down from heaven; therefore, nothing can happen to me unless it comes as an embrace of love. Love is the end of all. Heaven is love because God is love; God is heaven.

I like to look at God this way when kneeling at the crib: Jesus came to manifest His love. Why did He wish to show me His love? Because love is the most attractive power in the universe.

He wants my love. Why does He want my love? To make me happy. He knows that I can not be happy outside Himself, the Sovereign Good.

I must not go beyond two pages, Sister. Let us renew our pact.

What has a Trappist, but Jesus and Mary here, but especially in heaven?

Have your little ones pray for me.

In Jesus and Mary,
fr. M. Gerard O.C.S.O.

Gerard's notes and letters to the family indicated that he really loved his life in the monastery.

Our Lady of Gethsemani
January 5, 1944

Dear Ev and Joe,

Your letters and gift were received and enjoyed on the feast. I ask our dear Lord, whose nature is to give, to reward you for being so much like Himself. God is love, and love is diffusive; that is why Jesus told us it is more blessed to give than to receive. Maybe some time when I collect my thoughts I'll talk over with you the beautiful, because true, way of viewing God in creation, redemption and sanctification — the way of love. He created, etc., to give, not to receive.

I have so many verities which do me good that I would like you to share with me. Our Mystical Mass is one of these. I'll outline it sometime and then perhaps enlarge on it in "*tempore opportuno.*" That Mystical Body with all its ramifications warms me up very much; in fact, it delights me. I am going into it more this year if Jesus and Mary see fit to give me health and time. If I only had the love for study in my youth that I am acquiring in my old age, I might have persuaded some of those former students to go beyond the grades.

After all, to study God whether in Himself or in His handiwork is the very *raison d'etre* of our existing at all. That is why the prophet complains that people have gone astray and are halting off into byways instead of keeping mind and will traveling with accelerated pace down the great illumined speedway of knowledge and love of the *Summum Bonum*, God.

. . . I hope that you have informed all the family to begin the First Fridays on January 7. The bond will be put away for maturity. The other two Masses sent on December 5 I did not reply to because I did not get the letter until Christmas.

I do hope the promise of the Sacred Heart will be fulfilled in us all, that we might die in His good pleasure and fortified with the graces and sacraments of holy Church.

Sister Myron made a rather unwelcome remark. She felt someone of the family will die soon. I pray to God that "soon" means twenty years or more — Bill would be seventy then. God has blessed our family indeed, no sickness to amount to anything, etc.

I want God to please Himself above all, but I feel that I could love and suffer a bit more before I go.

Some way or other I feel I am drawing a bit nearer to Him — I mean in a love way. Creatures seem to play less in my life; I mean, my eye runs quicker to our Lord to see if He be pleased or displeased rather than, "What do men think?" My vocation, too, is dearer and dearer to me even though the cross remains as it always will. It is only by loving Him and proving my love by suffering for Him that I find solace and comfort. Unless my disposition would change immensely, I could never find joy in creature comforts, in worldly delights.

That merging into Jesus distills into one's soul so gradually and so slowly, if one be faithful, that the transformation is not perceived until years have fled. That little prayer mother taught us in the childhood of our lives is becoming more dear to me daily. "Live, dearest Jesus, so live in me that I might always live in Thee, and grant that all I think, do, or say, may be done by Thee this day." "All for Jesus; all for Jesus." What more do we need?

I have a little sermon I'll send to you. I am sending one to Sister Myron which I will tell her to send to you.

Here I am at the end. You both are daily in Holy Mass, three times on Christmas, and my New Year's Mass was for you.

God bless you all year through and Mary love you.

In Jesus and Mary,
fr. M. Gerard

Our Lady of Gethsemani
January 6, 1944

Dear Ag, Ed, and All:

Christmas has glided over our Kentucky knolls, delved down and caressed us and passed on into 1944, leaving us happy, blessed, and peaceful. I whispered to Jesus that He be as sweet and gift-giving to you. He promised.

Your Christmas was a much happier one than many throughout the world. How many children are deprived of the sweets of Christmas because their daddies and rulers do not want Christ. This year is God's year, and His plans will work out this year just as they have for the past thousands of years. Individually and collectively we are smaller than we suspect. God cannot act for an imperfect end; therefore, it behooves us to get into the swing and sway of His divine plans if we want a perfect year — if we want to be peaceful, happy, and holy.

"Peace is the tranquillity of order." Providence is the mind and will of God regulating and ordering all things to an end known to Himself. So I am the maker of my year, my peace, my happiness. If I but ally myself with the divine order, I will have peace; I will have the tranquillity resulting from tending toward my end which is happiness — the happiness of knowing and loving God. That is why I have a mind to know truth and infinite truth, and a will to love, and to love the sovereign good. When I stop at a creature, I find no peace, no rest, for I am made for the infinite. I must order all accordingly.

Well, I must not run on.

I received Kathleen's, Ann's, and Jack's* letter sometime ago.

* The Lavelle children.

I congratulate them all. I'll write them some day. . . .
Greetings and every blessing for this New Year.

In Jesus and Mary,
fr. M. Gerard

By 1944, Gethsemani's walls were about to burst with new recruits. The contemplative life had made an impact on the minds of young Americans.

The Abbot and community realized that it was necessary to make a new foundation. In a letter to his brothers and sisters, Father Gerard told of the departure of twenty monks and brothers to found a new monastery in Conyers, Georgia.

Our Lady of Gethsemani
May 20, 1944

My dear Brothers and Sisters All:

I put off our Easter letter writing to collect our thoughts, but as there is no sign of a coalescing yet, I might just as well go on with my usual dearth.

Is it too late to wish you Easter happiness? Perhaps. Then let me wish you the joys of the Resurrection and Ascension, for we are still in the Paschal season and Jesus has been spreading His joy abroad and blessing the earth, even the warring nations, with His wounded but gloriously triumphant hands. For the mysteries of Jesus are not merely historical events but are taking place *now* in souls.

Even though I had stood at the foot of the cross on that first Good Friday, I would have shared and participated in that world-saving death by grace only. So, we are equally blessed and more blessed than the faithful of Jesus' time; for we have more sureties of faith, especially the Resurrection, which those on Calvary did not have.

Jesus is with us now in His grace-laden humanity, glorious and immortal. "Christ has risen and will die no more." May He raise His divine hands over you during this season of pentecostal graces, in loving and bounteous benediction!

Jesus came to save us, indeed, but more to manifest God's love, His love, for us. He knows that love is the most attractive power in the universe; showing His love for me will attract my love in return.

Why does Jesus want my love? Has God any needs? He wants my heart because He knows I cannot be happy except in seeking and loving Him in all things, for He it is who fashioned me — my Creator, my God, the end of my being!

Peace results from a tranquillity of order, and thus I can rest happily only when my life and all my efforts and strivings are ordered to my proper end, to God, to Jesus.

Viewed in that manner, how good and sweet is God in commanding me to love Him with all my heart and strength and mind! It is *my* happiness that my dear heavenly Father is seeking when He bids me love Him and love all creatures in proper order: for His sake and not for themselves alone!

My soul aspires to the infinite; and when I stop at and rest in a lesser good, my intellect whispers to me that it is a creature, a participated good; it is finite and will not last; it has limits and cannot satisfy my longings; hence, the dissatisfaction and even disgust that is conceived in my will.

I suppose, fundamentally, we have here the reason why every Trappist is in the monastery: because we want to be happy.

Having allowed our looks and our loves to run down the many and varied avenues of life with its peaks and plains, our eyes were allured by our soul's longings; our hearts and our minds met with ends short of the infinite and therefore peace, rest, and happiness were not resultant.

We therefore turned aside from creatures, not because they were not good and very good, but because they were not good enough — they were not the Infinite Good.

Our intellects can rest perfectly in the Infinite Truth only, and our wills in the Infinite Good alone. Hence the joy of a life that aims at God alone.

You ask how can one be happy in a life of silence, solitude, and continual self-denial? Many answers might be given. I take this one:

It is a philosophical principle that the nearer one draws to the source of things, the more one participates in the properties of that source. Now God is the source of all true joy and happiness. . . . Therefore the nearer I draw to God by thought and affection, the more I participate in His own infinite bliss.

Thus our Trappist life of contemplation is one of the happiest of vocations.

Since the above has taken the form of a sort of apology for our mystical life, I might add that our life has its apostolic side also. It is a "redeeming" vocation. The only infallible means we have for the salvation of our own souls and the souls of others are prayer and penance (suffering), and these are precisely our life.

Well, my dear brothers and sisters, I was going to tell you something of our new daughterhouse, Our Lady of the Holy Ghost.

We have been feeling rather crowded here at Gethsemani for some time; thus there was talk of a foundation for a year or so.

Last February we bought a tract of land in Georgia, fourteen hundred acres. The crops were in, so we had to go to care for them.

On the feast of Saint Joseph, March 19, Reverend Father read out twenty names in chapter and announced that these twenty were to go to Georgia as founders of the new monastery. They had two days to prepare to leave their home of choice. Some [were] here for forty years. This, of course, meant that they were to depart and never see or be seen again by their brothers of Gethsemani.

Supernatural love is stronger and more tender than natural love, and that truth was brought home to us strongly when they left for Georgia.

On the eve (after Benediction) of the feast of Saint Benedict, a feast of tears, they gathered in the church, and we said some prayers for them: "The prayers for those who go on a journey."

They took their collation (Lent). From then until their final leave, the time was spent in farewells. The priests exchanged blessings and the others a kiss of peace. All was done in silence and tears.

The question is often asked: how can you love each other

when you do not speak, for love comes from knowledge? Well, I can't explain just how it is, but if pain in parting with a beloved one denotes love, then I have never experienced nor witnessed such fraternal charity as from the 19th to the eve of the 21st of March!

To depart from dear ones with the hope of a renewed meeting in a year or five years is something, but to say goodbye forever — oh, that hurts.

We accompanied them to the door of the monastery, and they rolled away to the railroad station in five cars.

They had their bed clothing, mattresses, etc., in a mountainous heap at the station. Reverend Father asked that the train stop a half hour to load, but they only granted ten minutes, as it was a passenger train. So all our neighbors were at the station, and together with the religious, they did one-half hour's work in seven minutes; then the train was off for Georgia.

Strange to say there were very few tears at the gate. To see those men going off smiling and with lights in their eyes was an inspiration that will last a long time! One said he found it easy, for it was "all for Jesus."

The religious with Father Abbot occupied a part of the car. The other part had the bedding. They said their Office in two choirs. They *sang* the *Salve Regina*. And it just happened that they were in the middle of the *Salve* when the train stopped at a station. The people must have asked if there were movie actresses on the train. (They like to "pull stuff.")

They arrived at Georgia (Atlanta) and were surrounded by cameras. They didn't dare face any of them. All the priests of the town were there.

They arrived at their *barns*. They had altar stones with them, and by three o'clock they were saying Mass — ten priests and Reverend Father. They left Gethsemani at 6 p.m.; Atlanta, 8 a.m.; at the monastic barn at 10. They are still living in the barn. Father James said the very roosters are aiding the K.K.K. to get the monks out; for on Easter Saturday when we begin our mid-day siesta, a group of the fittest and with the most powerful vocal cords arrayed themselves before their hayloft dormitory and began in a high pitch their premature Alleluias as best they could crow them. No sleep for the poor monks.

Reverend Father received a letter from the subprior yesterday, and he said that he (the subprior) and the father master of the lay brothers, both priests, were plowing every day. I thought that ought to make some of the followers of Nazareth's Carpenter turn red. It pepped me up so much that I felt like throwing a harness on the first mule I met, that I might not be outdone in humility and generosity.

Here all is May flowers, birds, song, sunshine, and glory — the earth bathed and laved in Heaven's bliss. . . .

I have thousands of thoughts yet, but I better end here. Reverend Father will turn a somersault in his abbatial chair if I add a fifth page.

Let us live and die as saints, my dear brothers and sisters.

In Jesus and Mary, Queen of the May,
fr. M. Gerard, O.C.S.O.

On January 2, 1945, Father Gerard wrote: The main thing, Sister, is that we ourselves grow like Jesus. I believe I do want Him as much and more than I ever did. I guess it is a question of things beginning to wave before my dimming eyes. I rejoiced more this Christmas season that I left the world than ever before. When the world is returning to bed from the night before, we enter choir and sing *Gloria Patri.* How blessed we are! God's every action is directed to overcoming our reluctance to receive Him. When we reject lesser goods and choose Him, He comes. To want Jesus!

For me there is only one big thing ahead — eternity. Eternity will be a wonder for all; what will it be for a Trappist?

You know, Sister, as religious, our aim is the apex of love. There is no real love without union of wills, and perfect union of wills is perfect love.

It is not our work that our Lord needs, Sister, but our wills — not our hands, but our hearts.

I gave a few retreats to priests this year, but I was not the retreat master of the year. This year . . . I am reappointed, so you know what that means. . . . I count so fully on prayer for any good the retreats might bring. . . .

After serving as guestmaster, retreat master, and infirmarian, Father Gerard was next appointed master of lay brothers. "One of the brothers wished me a Happy New Year, with many crosses," *Father said.* "He had crosses all over the paper."

In his letters in 1946, Father Gerard often referred to his spiritual children.

Jan. 23, 1946

Dear Sister Myron:

I offered Holy Mass for your good Mother Mary Agnes. I asked all possible graces for her, and since she has been so good to you, Jesus must love her.

I am glad all goes well with you and the hospital.* The Mystical Body ought to reap much harvest for Jesus from it.

Reverend Father has gone to Georgia. Our new Prior gave his first explanation of the Rule in chapter this morning. He was like an old solitary. . . .

I am master of the lay brothers this year. I have to give four new talks every week. About two hundred a year. I fear I'll be all exhausted about June. We'll have to sing hymns, I suppose, from then on, novel though it might be.

Since I am writing to you, I'll say a bit more. I didn't care much for the appointment when I got it. But now I feel I'll like it very much. These good brothers are the cream of the monastery: simple, humble, good, and full of one love. They could hardly have self-love and be Trappist Brothers. Their life is not sacrificial; it is a sacrifice. There is no cessation.

One assured me the only motive that urges him is to make Jesus smile—all to please Him. Here is perfect love!

One [brother] likes to go "fishing." When he feels a "fish" [a sacrifice] in the net (Trappists don't catch water fish) he draws it in for Jesus.

Another says he likens himself to a little dog. He generally contemplates the sweet countenance of Jesus, but when Jesus indicates a sacrifice, he runs out and gets it and brings it back to Jesus.

---

* Sister Myron was assigned to Ogden during the construction of St. Benedict's Hospital.

Remember me on January 30th, the great Blessed Gerard's feast day. If you wish to read about him, read Sermon Twenty-six on the "Canticle of Canticles" of St. Bernard.

God bless you. Happy Valentine's Day!

In Jesus, Mary, Joseph,
fr. M. Gerard, O.C.S.O.

May 10, 1946

My dear Sister Elaine:

May the sweetest peace of our dear Lord inundate your good soul, my dear Sister Elaine.

Father Gerard forgotten you? How could he forget the one who taught him to fold his hands and to say for the first time those words which he now says with his folded anointed hands: *Introibo ad altare Dei?* You are in my Mass intention *aliter* every day. God bless you, Sister. It was your goodness and sweetness that made Jesus so alluring. You were the spark that led me to His fiery Heart.

I was so late in our Christmas correspondence that I passed beyond our writing season. Hence this is in answer to your Christmas letter. You are the only one outside the family, except Leo, whom you know, with whom I exchange words. When I ask Reverend Father to write you, I tell him it was you who gave me my vocation. He feels he ought not refuse in that case!

Yes, I gave retreats last year. We never had so many priests on retreat — about three or four hundred, besides retreats, about every week — sometimes twice a week — for laymen.

I appreciate more than I can say your little ones' prayers. One man came five hundred miles; he was forty years out of the Church. . . . I asked him, "Did you ever say a prayer to Mary?"

He reached in his pocket and pointed to a May prayer to Mary. "Father," he said, "I've said that prayer every day." Our Mother! One can do so much good for those poor men. One, a Protestant, had determined to take his life. A man brought him to a retreat. I talked to him in public and private, and he went home singing, a new vision in his soul. Another was found committing suicide. His folks brought him for a retreat. He made a good resolve never to drink again, went out, and was back in three weeks. He had failed flatly. I "put the bee on him" stronger than ever. . . . He is playing the game and is very happy ever since.

A priest (it had been thirty-one years since his last confession) said Mass every day. I was never so edified as when he bathed the crucifix before him with his tears. What joy there must have been in the Sacred Heart at that conversion! He did mean what He said, "I am the Good Shepherd." How good Jesus is. He works miracles today just as He did in Judea.

Dear Sister, since you are mother and sister both, I speak freely; retreat work is most interesting when I am in it, but when out of it I have no desire to go back. The Trappist life when lived to the core is so sweet; the core of Trappist life is Jesus, He is in me and I in Him, with Mary. Love is sweet and love is joy-giving. That is just what our life is if it be anything at all — love. All for Jesus, all for Jesus.

Today is the feast of our Lady of the Smile. How I love that dearest of Mothers. So sweet, so fair, so motherly and maternally thoughtful. My love is not always followed out in generous service, I fear. Even though I fail, she still keeps her loving eyes upon me. I so often feel the love-throbbings of her sweet motherly heart as she caresses me from time to time even when I do not deserve it — she must see Jesus in me and loves me as she did her boy at Nazareth.

Today is the one hundredth anniversary of the dedication of the United States to Mary Immaculate. It makes me happy to be in Kentucky even though its sun rays burn with purgatorial fury. A slogan could be: "Go to Kentucky to avoid purgatory." We've got to be prepared for the heavenly banquet; one way is to be roasted and toasted in Kentucky's bright sun. In winter we are frozen into a sort of delicacy — a spiritual ice cream — in the divine eyes; thus, too, are we prepared for that banquet. I hope to get a seat near you, Sister. I cannot say half in these small pages how alluringly sweet [the prospects of] those meetings in heaven seem. What will they be for a Trappist?

Oh, dear Sister, pray for me, won't you, that I never fail Jesus in this holy life. It is such a glory, and such an unmerited call to be a Trappist — to give one's all for the All. As a novice

I did not at times appreciate our life of entire stripping, but I have learned it is only when by mortification, self-love has been killed, that Jesus grows large in one's soul and attractively lovable. I would love Him so; Mary, too — my Mother, my Queen, my Lady, my Spouse; we will see her someday with our bodily eyes, be caressed by her and kneel and kiss her virginal hand. . . . My spiritual sons are so loving and good — how many stories I could tell you. One just brought in a rose with a card: "My lady is a fragrant rose, and near to God my Lady grows."

You may wonder what I mean by my spiritual sons. I am master of the brothers this year. I have thirty-six brothers to direct, guide, and instruct. Many of them are saints. One put flowers all over our desk for our feast day. I thanked him in the evening, and very naïvely he said, "Oh, I didn't do it for you; I did it for Jesus." Isn't that splendid?

One was holding his hand on the barn wall and a truck hit his hand and smashed it. I said, "What did you say when the truck hit your hand?" "Thanks, Jesus." This is the kind of brothers I have.

One brought a letter; he said, "May I burn this?" I replied, "Better let me read it to see if anything of moment is in it."

"Oh, I have already burned several — I wanted to read them so badly," he admitted.

. . . Above all, Sister, offer your actions to Jesus. I like to say at my chief actions: "All for and with you, Jesus and Mary," meaning "All for your intentions and with your dispositions." This is the most meritorious intention we can have. This is where our love and money lie — in our intention. I make it about fifty times a day — at every chief change in the day. Trappists have a good many turnings, not only from the world and from self toward God, but ten times a day in Church, and then at our other exercises.

Sister Myron is scrubbing floors in her new hospital. The first training in hospital work is scrubbing floors. I guess that she will stay there; she seems glued to Utah; she can't even come to Kentucky for a family reunion. . . . I have two robes worn out praying for her, and every letter urges more hours and longer litanies — all for the hospital.

Reverend Father is in France — flew over. Trappists are going up! He will be back on May 18. A special general chapter was held this year. . . .

. . . Good little Sister, God bless you and keep you ever in His love.

The family is well. All were here last fall except Sister Myron. Syl is married and has a splendid little wife, pious and good.

Sweet Mary, Jesus love,
fr. M. Gerard

Nov. 3, 1946

My dear Brothers and Sisters:

Greetings *in Domino* from Kentucky.

All is well away down here in Dixieland. The weather is autumnal. The trees on the knolls decked in green, red, and gold are dancing heel and toe to the music of the southern breezes. . . . It all whips one's soul to the heights, to the praises of God. And when our souls are once in tune we find our jubilee in the eternal joys.

The saints in whose octave we are seem to beam upon us amid all this fall splendor.

There are few feasts so cheering as All Saints' Day. It recalls the dogma of the communion of saints. We may not be quite what we ought to be, but our brothers and sisters are; and we share in all their beauties and virtues.

This is our real "family feast." All are feasted — Father (God); Mother (Mary); and the angels and saints (our brothers and sisters).

This family, or Mystical Body, has a great treasury — the merits of Jesus, Mary, and all the saints. "I believe in the communion of saints." This means that each one participates in the goods of the others. I have what they have, and they have what I have. According to the principle: "If I love the good that is in my neighbor more than he himself loves it, that good is more mine than his"; for in spiritual things, it is love that gives possession. Just as a person is not *my friend* unless I *love* him.

So love is the "open sesame" to this infinite treasure. By being the heart (lovers) in Mother Church, I open the sluice gates of heaven and torrents of love pent up in the Mystical Body rush into our souls, consuming them with love. This is how the Little Flower thought of becoming a victim of love.

What is love? St. Thomas says it is doing the will of the beloved. Therefore, as long as I keep my resolve firm — to please Jesus in everything — I keep the gates to love's treasury wide open to my own soul and its golden waters flood the whole world because of my key to love.

As this is winter time and you have longer hours for reading, we might ask again, what is love? Love in its most generic sense is an impulse of the soul towards good. If the good be appealing to sense-nature (as an apple or a hug) and our imagination feels it agreeable, it is sensible or feeling love. If the good presented is a moral good, acknowledged by reason as worthy of esteem (as a good character, a clever thinker, etc.) it is a rational love. If the good is supernatural, perceived by faith (as to esteem all men as children of God or because Jesus said: "Whatever you do to them you do to me," or to prefer Holy Communion to a grandiose wedding feast, etc.) it is Christian love and charity.

In all love there is a sympathy — there need not be a likeness always, because often opposites attract because of the need of completion, e.g., a tall husband will love his short wife or vice versa or a fat wife will have as her dearest a very thin little fellow. Then there is an impulse, a tending to draw near to, to enjoy the presence of the loved object. Also a communion or sharing of the goods of mind and heart — conversation and expressing of affection. Lastly, a sense of joy in possessing the object loved, although in this world hope often gives more joy than does possession. A lady was asked what was the happiest day of her life? She said, "the day before." But this will not be true of heaven. The possession will not be of the finite only but of the infinite.

Dogmatically, charity is a supernatural virtue causing us to love God for His own sake and our neighbor for God's sake, and God above all.

When self-love is condemned we only refer to inordinate self-love, the love that goes contrary to God's will.

Charity is the most excellent and sanctifying of virtues. It is the essence of perfection to which all are called. "Be ye perfect as your heavenly Father is perfect," not in degree but in kind by grace which is a participation in God's nature.

Charity unites the whole soul to God: the mind through esteem and thought of Him; the will by perfect submission of our will to His; the heart by subordination of our affections to divine love. It makes us wish to be like Jesus, like God, and actually effects what we wish. Love keeps us steadfast, "Love is as strong as death."

True charity is productive of great joy and expansion of soul. You often hear the cry by daring youth, "I want life; I want love." This is really a yearning for God. God is life — all life comes from Him. God is love. Love (supernatural) puts me in possession of the Sovereign Good; therefore, it is the beginning of eternal life. Hence, its overflowing joy — to be with Jesus is a sweet paradise.

Charity gives peace. Peace is the tranquillity of order; hence, I do all for Jesus (for love) and accept all from Jesus (from love); then peace is mine here and oh, what hereafter!

How can I make progress in love, in charity?

Ascetically love is a gift of self. Now the only way I can give myself to a spiritual being is through my spiritual faculties: mind and will. Therefore, I draw near to God — I become happy. I give myself to Him by thought and affection — by doing His holy will. I can only do His will habitually by sacrificing my own will; therefore, the more sacrifice the more love. This means a preference of His will to mine.

Sin is a turning from God and turning to the creature, so I must be . . . turned [far enough] toward God as not to be entirely sod-bent.

Patience is the barometer which infallibly tells me where I am spiritually. For I can be patient only when I see all as God's will or permission and submit perfectly to Him. And this is perfection, perfect conformity to God's will. This is what the saints teach us — love; and love is the key to love's treasury.

The pages are flying by; better stop here lest I run by reasonable limits for respectable monks.

Rev. Father is in the West right now.

We have had many abbots here of late because of the two blessings in Georgia, our daughter house, and Iowa our sister house. We are all one family. There were two abbots from Ireland and one from Canada and Dom Edmund from the East. We expect one from France any day.

Everything is well here. A new foundation is in the offing—next March about. In a monastery where there are vows of stability, it means more than just passing to another house. We have about sixty-five novices now. One physician among them, fourteen priests-novices—all putting on the Lord Jesus. They are sainting their souls unto eternal glory.

I just told the brothers in conference: we are here in the dressing room of the heavenly marriage banquet (speaking about the man not having on the wedding garment) getting all togged up in grace by prayer and penance, so that neither lilies nor roses will be wanting.

It is too bad you didn't all become Trappists when you were of a younger growth. No, Madeline, you cannot get out of it, just because Trappists are men—we are having Trappistines soon in the U. S. . . .

Advent is near. If we put a little more love and sacrifice and a few more Communions into it, it will bloom into a sparkling and heaven-kissed Merry Christmas. May Jesus from the arms of Mary bless you all now and on holy Christmas day. You are in my Masses and my mystic Mass.

Merry Christmas to you all.
Your brother the Trappist,
fr. M. Gerard

Letters from Father Gerard in 1947 seemed to point to two special interests: the first, love of the Sacred Heart of Jesus, of which he spoke and wrote often; and the second, an interest in another foundation for the monastery. The Abbot wanted to establish a house where there were few Catholics. Gethsemani had continued to attract new recruits. Young men who had been in the armed services, and others who had experienced the world and found it wanting, flocked to the monastery. Many of them found the life strenuous and exacting, but not beyond endurance;

they gave themselves to prayer and work, and persevered. Others lacked stability and returned home, better men for having experienced life in a twentieth-century monastery.

Father Gerard suggested Utah as a possible site for a new foundation. He wrote to his sister inquiring about the weather in winter and summer; he asked about the crops, the water supply, the grazing land for cattle, and about the fruits and vegetables grown there. Sister Myron, who was in Ogden, where the Sisters of St. Benedict were constructing a new hospital, sent word to the Bishop of Salt Lake, Duane G. Hunt, of the possibility of Gethsemani's Trappists making a new foundation soon. Almost immediately the Bishop invited Abbot Frederic to the diocese to examine property which might be desirable for the projected monastery. The sites first offered did not suit Dom Frederic. However, before long, Monsignor Wilfrid J. Giroux, pastor of St. Joseph's Church, Ogden, located a large tract of land a few miles from Huntsville, Utah, which satisfied the Abbot, who purchased it without delay.

The next few letters give an insight into the monk's special interests.

Jan. 14, 1947

My dear Brothers and Sisters:

Are seasonal greetings still in order? I have wished you all possible goods at the earliest hour on Christmas day and on New Year's, too. What is wished in God's ear, in the ear of Jesus, is worth more than a penned word. You were present with me at my three Christmas Masses. I have so arranged now that whatever I do, you do also. Jesus is too good to divide my little works. So you all have the whole of my Mass, Office, etc. St. Alphonsus says that one hour spent in the confessional is worth two hours spent in adoration before the Blessed Sacrament. So I add five or six hours of daily adoration. Once we seminarians were discussing what work we would like best in the ministry. I thought I'd like the confessional. Jesus is good to me.

Our festivities passed off with their usual joy-giving grandeur. Mother Church and our Cistercian Mother take good care of us.

At Christmas it was cool enough, and fair. But just before Christmas we had a thunderstorm, and a few days ago it thundered again. Will winter come? Our Kentucky weather does not believe in the tranquillity of order, where peace lies. Our Lord thought our bright sun would impart enough joy. Right here in Nelson County they don't think so; for most of these knoll-dwellers have joy-supplies in their cellars.

It would be a good thing to make the nine Fridays as a family again this year. We'll start on the first Friday of February the 7th. I'll say Mass for you all. . . . Let no one miss those Fridays. Communion, Mass — and can't we add a rosary for the family on the first Saturday of the month? The Blessed Virgin appearing at Fatima asked that her Immaculate Heart be honored by a rosary on the first Saturday of the month. "Holy Mary, Mother of God, pray for us now and at the hour of our death." How beautiful and necessary!

There was a man here this summer who told me that for some years they had set Thursday aside as "Family Day." He has a priest and a nun and a doctor in his family. So we will take Friday for Mass and Communion and Saturday for the rosary. There are none [of you] out in the country, so why shouldn't these months be as good as any? If one would fail to communicate on the first Friday for some very serious reason, then let him not fail on the following Sunday.

And why couldn't we make this a continual chain? When one set of nine ends, we begin another? This one will end in October. I hope you will all try to communicate every week or oftener, but don't miss the first Friday. Or, as I said, if one would miss, then the following Sunday will make good for this family agreement.

My dear brothers and sisters, we must help each other to get through this life unscathed and to reach a happy family reunion in heaven. If any one of us were dying of hunger, all the others would help. Now, any one of us may need a lot of aid even before death, or at least in the hour of death, to avoid the pitfalls of self-love and those which the devil lays for us. So let us all join hands, that loving each other with true affection on earth, we may be one mind and one heart with God and our dear ones in eternity.

Let no one miss the Saturday rosary (the family rosary) from now until death.

What will the intentions be? These intentions, of course, include all sisters-in-law and brothers-in-law and Bill's and Ag's families.

1. A happy death for all.
2. A holy life — avoiding mortal sin.
3. That the bond of family love be never broken.
4. Prosperity in material matters according as God wills it, and is for our best.
5. That through the holy Mass we might ever be united with all the "goods" of the Mystical Body and live and die clothed with the plenitude of love.
6. All your personal and private intentions.

We might as well face matters squarely and advise ourselves rightly: we have not here a lasting dwelling. Let's seek realities!

A heart full of affection and good wishes to everyone of you. May Mary and her Child, the God of love, bless us and keep us in peace and in charity of soul.

Pray for a little project I have in view.

Your little brother,
fr. M. Gerard

April 12, 1947

Dear Sister Myron:

The holy Monsignor Giroux is here. I saw him at his request the other day for a short time. He went down to Georgia with Reverend Father and the Abbot General. He, the Monsignor, has a good, a very good reputation at Gethsemani. Brother Giles is a bit of an architect, and Brother Clement is an engineer; they are drawing up plans for the Utah foundation. . . . Brother Clement remarked that Monsignor is simple, very level-headed, zealous, and pious — enough encomiums, I think, for any saint. He left again for sunny Utah.

We had our regular visitation. It always leaves peace and fraternal love in its wake.

Our General is a glorious man, a born Trappist!

Our spring is much later than yours, according to Monsignor. But when our spring does come, one can neither study, read, nor apply oneself to earthly affairs. One can only sing and praise Him whose beauty lies heavily over our graceful knolls.

Brother Godfrey, from St. Paul, made his profession last Sunday. I now have him as a spiritual son. He is one of the most loving characters I've ever met. He studied for the priesthood for years, knows his Latin, Greek, German, and French. He teaches me French. I'm getting so I can say "hello" and a couple other things in French. The future looks hopeful, doesn't it? I'm letting German go. French is our Order language. I can read, but oh, the speaking. Reverend General speaks English but very poorly. He couldn't catch much of my French nor I much of his English. Yet all the words were in our minds.

As for Utah—who is going? We have no certainty as yet. Reverend Father would make a splendid pope. He never divulges a secret.

Keep up your good prayers that God's will be done and that we all submit to and embrace that will with love.

I am reading a little pamphlet, "In the School of Jesus" by Karg, O.S.B. . . . I've often told the brothers to have a motto and an ejaculation, and hold to it. Father Karg calls it "The Little Secret." I like the name. It works into love.

In Jesus and Mary,
fr. M. Gerard, O.C.S.O.

July 4, 1947

Dearest Sister Myron:

I'm celebrating the 4th with you. We have chocolate in the morning and some candy at noon, and two nuts, and we thus end all external celebration.

So you've been praying for a special intention these days? Must I tell you that Jesus has not deigned to hear your prayer?

About the day you receive this letter, the Trappist battalion of thirty-four will be pulling into Ogden to inaugurate their battle against the wicked spirits in high places. You will recognize one face, maybe two — but Father Gerard will not be with them. Did you expect him? Did he expect to go? Did he want to go? I might as well tell you all.

I did want to go, naturally, and I expected it for some time, as the whole community did.

When you gave my Easter letter to Monsignor Giroux, he wrote to the bishop, as Monsignor told me, and the bishop wrote to Reverend Father. Reverend Father called the council (I happen to be on it), and things began moving.

Well, when I saw I was in some wise the instigator of the project, I thought it best to step back and let God work as He wanted; so I said little or nothing about it. This may have made Reverend Father think I was not enthusiastic.

A few days after Georgia was established, a confrere and I were agreeing that in a few years we would be in the Rockies. And even then I thrilled at the prospect.

The opinion in the community that I was going was so general that several came and asked me if I would take them under my wing as I flew across country. That pleased me more than I wished them to know. About four or five months ago I saw I was not going, and I felt that very keenly.

Why did I wish to go to Utah? Well, very humbly, I'll have to say, I believe it was the call of the wild. It was to help . . . yes, but I can do that right here in Gethsemani. I believe the big incentive was the thrill of adventure. Then, too, I suffer from sinus, and especially from some kind of throat infection. I'm something like old man Jarr [a neighbor]; I have to clear my throat before any vocalization can be produced. . . . It's a sort of laryngitis or something allied to it. We are very low [in elevation] here, a little over one hundred to three hundred above sea level, hence much throat and chest trouble.

. . . I am celebrating the Passover of perhaps my great natural desire. Jesus, it is all for You. I have been resting in Jesus' will for sometime. I needed that haven of repose, to be found nowhere else. By uniting my will with His, He aided me so as not to offend Him in this, I hope; and, too, I did not feel the departure nearly as much as the Georgia one, although today is sepulchral!

Some changes of officers were made, and because of the shortage, some have extra loads. I find myself holding two burdensome, time-occupying positions. I have the brother novices, and I am infirmarian again. Our infirmarian went to Utah. I always thought it would be splendid to be novice master, but when one gets right into the boat, one realizes better what rowing means. I do enjoy the novices very much, and it will be a powerful urge to sanctify my soul. "For them do I sanctify myself." I am giving Jesus and Mary the heavier end of my onus, and like St. Thérèse, I'll not turn my head from Him when feeding His lambs. Both positions ought to be excellent for my soul. Little Thérèse desired to be infirmarian, and she'll be my big aid and real sister in caring for the novices. Her little way will be their way, for it is mine. I count on your prayers now.

The pioneers left last evening, the 7th, at eight o'clock. We all saw them to the gate and farwelled them in perfect silence. It was the great silence, night silence. They have two cars, one freight and one passenger. They got in at Gethsemani and will get out at Ogden. There are thirty-four and Reverend Father. . . . The superior will most probably be Father Mauritius. The community will be formed out there. I will send this by air so it will be there before them. They are to be two days and three nights on the train. . . .

In Jesus and Mary,
fr. M. Gerard

"Our novitiate is increasing," *Father Gerard wrote late in November, 1947.* "We have twenty-eight — the largest number in the history of Gethsemani. Splendid novices, too." *In a letter to his brothers and sisters, he described his joy in dealing with the young choir novices, his new charges.*

Spring, 1948

My dear Sisters and Brothers All,

I am much like the man in the gospel. . . . I say, I will, and behold, I don't. I have been two months edging down to this letter which is now in its beginning. Easter came with such a flash and suddenness that it took me off my feet, as it were, and I haven't been able to assume balance as yet, or I am just now balancing somewhat.

Many things have happened throughout the family since then. They have ranged from a change of town to occupation: Sister Myron, going from Utah to British Columbia and settling down there as a novice mistress of a religious order, or something to that effect; then graduations from high school as Jack and Ann [Lavelle] have just done; marriages both in Ryan and McGinley families; Ev and Joe have gone to New York to a convention this year. Syl, I believe, has not changed his address since Easter; Madeline is certainly exercising a beneficial influence upon him in a stabilizing way.

As for the monastery, things go on quite as usual. Reverend Father has gone out to Utah this past week in order to aid them by his counsel and to check on their progress in the material and spiritual order. He was down to Georgia not too long ago. They are rearing a gigantic and complete monastery. Indeed, they started on such a grandiose style, it is questionable whether our bank account, and those of our good benefactors, are going to stand up under the outpourings of expenditures. They have a large community down there — sixty already, and in Utah, they have forty. We are contemplating a new monastery to be founded shortly after our centenary, which will take place next spring, perhaps May.

I have just received a letter from Father Mauritius. (This will interest you, Sister Myron.) He tells me that they are the happiest group that one could imagine. He says that everything there is huge — the mountains are towering, the valleys are spacious, the crops are large, the rodents are plentiful, so plentiful, in fact, that as soon as they [the monks] plant anything in the garden, it is directly unplanted. But still he hopes by fences, cement walls, poisons, etc., some day to get the better of his mountaineer friends. He says he hopes to make $10,000 off of hay this year; that is beside what they need for their stock. In this way it will not take long to pay off their $100,000. The new foundation seems to be ideal, although it can freeze any month of the year. . . . Hay is their only staple crop, and it is a crop that they can handle very well because it lends itself to our manner of labor.

. . . There is a gentleman now in the hotel [the guest house] here who is from Utah, and he says that the weather was ideal — just like spring — while he was there during January and February. He might have sung a different song in July. We are not to divulge the place yet where the next monastery will be; our donors have requested this.

I was delighted, Sister Myron, at the long account of your journey. One of the novices wanted to read it to the novices on my birthday, but I promised him that he might do so another day. It is easy for you to understand some of the joys and sorrows which pass through the soul of one who has charge of other souls and especially when these are novice-souls. Our Lord has given me grace, though, not to worry. The virtue of trust has long been a beacon light which has attracted my soul so much so that trust has become one of the delightful virtues in which my soul finds its rest. I just ask Jesus and Mary to take over, and I sit back and enjoy their work in these little souls. I often praise them for their admirable condescension in hearing my prayer, and I delight in the marvels that they work in the most simple souls, and how they break down the complexity of other souls who need simplifying, so that their hearts may be like unto their own Sacred and Immaculate Hearts.

I have asked our novices to pray for your [Sister Myron's] novices, and I hope you will recommend our novices to them, that we might truly be one in Christ, having each other's interest at heart. If your novices have the virtues that are quite patent in the souls of our little ones, you will develop into a splendid Benedictine community.

I find, as doubtless you do, that the direction of others is a great aid to one's own spiritual uplift, for one is constrained to practice what he preaches, and thus where the novitiate requires almost daily preaching, it is a daily practice. Too, one has to rely so much on Our Lord that trust in His Sacred Heart and trust in our dear Mother is finally worn in one's soul. So in this sense it is a subject of thanksgiving to be given charge of souls, for it urges in a direct way to one's own soul's higher attainment.

I find that I must be a child again in all my concepts, resolutions, and outlooks. Monsignor Gay says that when we have a childlike eye toward God, we have very little more to do in the spiritual life. So don't forget me in prayer, and I'll include you, that our souls might so burn that their radiance will aid others because "No one gives what he does not have." Here it might be well to solicit the prayers of the family, too, that they might participate in all the good that will result to souls, and that good is apt to go on from year to year until it runs down into the eternal years of the everlasting society of the Mystical Body, and in the company of the Eternal Three where I hope we will all be found as one family, and the good of one will appear as the good of all.

. . . I must go to the hotel [guesthouse] to bring a postulant into the novitiate. He is a young man in his early thirties, who is setting his face toward Jerusalem to become a saint by living our life of prayer and penance. He is an x-ray technician, and he has several degrees; but we are receiving him because we hope he has the making of a saint.

I will be writing soon, and so I will leave you all in the loving Heart of Jesus and in the confidence-inspired heart of His holy Mother.

Ev is going to have you all write a short essay, thesis, sermonette on the Sacred Heart. Let no one renege when he is called on in this. It will increase the devotion of the writer as well as the reader and aid in the family interest.

Your little brother,
fr. M. Gerard

When he was giving retreats, Father Gerard published a small brochure on the Sacred Heart. It proved valuable to his retreatants, so he wrote to the family, suggesting that they write a short essay on the same subject. His object was to encourage the family to make the nine Fridays and to pray that Christ would be loved by all mankind. He wanted the theme to be entirely original. Apparently the family did not act as promptly as he expected, but he felt that the following letter would bring the desired results.

Trappist, Kentucky
1948

Dear Mary Ev,

A reprimand! I thought of marching you out on the carpet before the whole family, but I recall St. Benedict says that the first correction should be made *quasi in secreto* (between me and thee).

Now, when we launched the nine Fridays last, the urge was made to each and all to write an article, no less than 200 words, or two pages on the Sacred Heart. Each one of the family, Joe included, was — in my mind — to take a month and send the composition around the family.

Now, this has not been done. . . . The sticks (pens) are in your hands. Where goading is necessary, goading must be done. So I say, set to!

So may I urge that your thunderous suggestion to the family contain a proposal or program about like this:

1. One's own words are preferred to quoting.
2. Subject matter:
   a. My idea of devotion to the Sacred Heart. (This would be very interesting.)
   b. What the Sacred Heart has done for me.
   c. Why I make the nine Fridays.
   d. The goodness of the Sacred Heart.
   e. The mercy of the Sacred Heart.
   f. The Mass and the Sacred Heart.
   g. The Sacred Heart and the Blessed Sacrament.
   h. Christmas and the Sacred Heart.
   i. The Sacred Heart and Calvary.
3. Any one who fails to produce must finance the whole nine stipends for the next round of nine Fridays. . . .

. . . Appoint a subject or let them choose their own. But oh! be insistent. Maybe you have a typewriter which thunders and throws back lightning right into the face of the reader — use that machine. Anywise, I leave the dynamite in your hands; consult Joe, and then set the sparks going.

In you I place my hope — in you and Jesus and Mary.

fr. M. Gerard

The hearts of the Trappists were heavy on August 4, 1948, when a message announced the sudden death of their beloved Abbot Frederic Dunne, who expired on the train enroute to the Georgia monastery where he was to make a visitation. In the following letter, Father Gerard told of the death of their Abbot, and of the election of his successor, Dom James Fox.

Abbey of Gethsemani
Trappist, Kentucky
August 21, 1948

My dear Brothers and Sisters:

This is the Assumption of our dearest Mother and it brings with it a double joy, that of seeing Mary in glory with her Divine Son and a more earthly pleasure, that of again sending you a word of brotherly love and good wishes.

You have doubtless heard of the bereavement which has been ours since August 4, when by an eternal decree the time of our Reverend Father's sojourn upon earth came to an end. He died on the train on his way to Georgia. He was brought here, and we had the burial on August 9. We are now in the throes of an election and by Monday noon we will know who the new Abbot of Gethsemani will be. His position is hardly an enviable one, for if one opens the Rule of St. Benedict, he will be greeted by these words addressed to the abbot: "Let him know what a hard and onerous burden he has taken upon himself." That's why some of the saints used to run for miles in order to avoid being elected to the abbatial chair; however, someone must sit in it and fulfill the duties of abbot; and we are anxiously awaiting Monday morning to know who that one will be. The Father Immediate is a grand abbot. He towers high above us all. He is a perfect specimen of humanity, and he has a mind which complements his physique. He has been with us for three weeks, but he will return to France after the election. I spent the afternoon with him yesterday. He speaks only French; and of course, there were a few words that went over my head, but when he returns next time I hope to be able to understand every word he says.

For the election, all the superiors of our daughter houses will be present: Father Mauritius from Utah, Dom James from Georgia, and Dom Edmund from Rhode Island. We may choose from the abbots and superiors of our daughter houses, and it seems that Dom James has the preference right now; but we do not know what the Holy Ghost might have in view for us. A great wind from heaven might come into the chapter room on Monday morning and change the whole outlook of the voters — just as in the election of Cardinal Sarto, an obscure member of the College of Cardinals, who suddenly came to the fore and was finally elected, becoming Pius X. Few Popes have equalled him in either sanctity or wisdom.

Everything at the abbey is as usual with regard to our crops, etc. All the novices are in good spirits, and it is a relief for my mind when I can hand things over to Jesus and Mary completely. It gives me a sort of vacation. Sometimes they seem to wish that I partake in their act of charity, and they invite me to share the cross of uplifting their spirits from the mundane to the divine. Our senior novice will make his profession under the new abbot. With the blessing of God and the Blessed Virgin, we hope to have fifty novices by Christmas. If there is any radical change after election, I will let you know. However, the changes, whatever they will be, will only be in offices because we don't go places as Trappists, or only on very rare occasions, such as making new foundations.

I have just heard from Sister Myron that Ag is not well. I shall write her a line. I am making things a little short in this letter because our work in preparation for the election and installation of the new abbot is piling up, and I want to get it finished before it gets so high that I won't be able to get out from under it. . . .

We just celebrated the feast of St. Bernard, my patron saint. I asked him to bless you all as I do every day at Mass. I do hope that you will remember us during this time.

Your little brother in the Sacred Heart of Jesus,
fr. M. Gerard

P.S. Dom James of Georgia is our new Abbot. God bless him.

The Kentucky abbey began to celebrate its centennial shortly before Christmas in 1948. The actual celebration, however, took place in 1949.

Our Lady of Gethsemani
Trappist, Kentucky
January 8, 1949

My dear Brothers and Sisters,

Here we are at another Christmas Day. The bells and carols are all in jubilant mood; they are wafting the glad tidings of the Savior's birth far and near. Even our knolls, right here in far-off Kentucky, have sensed the spirit of the times and are swinging and swaying in sweet melodies and rhapsodies of joy and glee. Every Kentucky colonel is showing his blue blood by gallantly greeting every on-comer with the loftiest greetings of the season.

Our Christmas here in the monastery was undoubtedly and beyond compare the most grandiose and solemn and jubilantly gleeful of any we have ever had at Gethsemani.

We started to celebrate in a family way our centennial on December 21, for that was the day our holy fathers arrived at Gethsemani. We had the archbishop and other dignitaries here. [There was] singing, decorations, and a monastic play giving the history of our abbey down through the last hundred years. It was all very unique and gratifying to each of us. We left the decorations up over the Christmas holidays and so our chapter room and refectory were decorated as never before for Christmas. To top it off with something that we never dreamed of before in the monastery, we had Handel's "Messiah" played during refectory meals.

All seems so homelike. I was carried back to the old Viking* days when you, my dear ones and I, were young. . . .

I was just recalling those Farrell-McGinley Christmases, the first of my recollections. And the very first one was the most disastrous; for it was the one on which I fell into Johnnie's** tank.

* The name of the settlement in which the McGinleys and Farrells lived.
** Farrell's tank was used by the children for skating, but the ice was too thin.

I recall Raphael's* "Merry Christmas, Merry Christmas" unto hoarseness. The sleigh bells, the sleds and cutters, the deep snow on the fields and hanging in ermine streaks and crystals from the trees, the horses' frosty breath, the silent, holy-night stillness with but an occasional distant bark of some shepherd dog was a perfect Christmas setting. How my heart used to fill and surge and sort of swoon away in reveries, as the sweet notes of Christmas carols surged in upon my perfectly attuned spirit. Oh! some day I will have to sit down and let our pen run and roam through the snow drifts and sweet dreams of Viking Christmases. The fairy-like beauties and charms of childhood memories will certainly sweeten our eternal ecstasies.

Here at Gethsemani all is quiet after the Christmas holidays. . . . The novices were gleeful in their spiritual joys as well as with their Christmas cards and letters. You can hardly imagine what a Trappist Christmas is like. It is really Jesus in His crib at Bethlehem, surrounded by Mary and Joseph and His chosen few. I would not trade a Trappist Christmas for all the glares and gleams that New York could possibly offer.

I must close now, for the mailman is at the door. I leave you all in the protective love of Jesus and Mary at the crib.

Your little brother,
fr. M. Gerard

June 7, 1949

Dear Brothers and Sisters,

This letter will come as a surprise.** We all have received permission to write concerning the centenary jubilee. It was indeed a unique affair, such as has never been seen amidst these Kentucky knolls and perhaps will not be seen for some years to come.

First of all, we spent a long time . . . preparing our singing, sending our invitations, painting coats of arms for the bishops, building the altar and various other accessories. The day before the jubilee, the bishops and abbots began to arrive. When the

---

* Gerard's cousin.
** Permission for special letters was needed by Trappists.

novices and I returned from New Haven* with a load of chairs, we just arrived in time to greet Cardinal Dougherty, Archbishop Floersch, and Bishop Buddy as they arrived at the door. . . . Archbishop Floersch had all the little children come over to kiss the Cardinal's ring. It was late at night when we got the last touches on the jubilee display. In fact, we had all the farm animals and implements out in the avenue on display. Father Simon, one of the novices, had to take his bees out after dark. New Haven took care of the hot dog stands and Coca-Cola fountains. I never saw so many Coca-Cola bottles in all my life, strewn over the fields and sidewalks when we came to pick them up the next day. The reason for the hot dog and Coca-Cola stand was that the people who stayed for Benediction in the afternoon would not then be too oppressed with hunger. It was impossible for us to provide for 25,000 dinners. At it was, we served about 750 dinners in the interior of the monastery. The Kentucky hotel men took over in the refectory. There were about twenty men, so we were relieved on that score. We had tables in our refectory and all around the cloisters. The community ate in other rooms wherever there was sitting space.

The day dawned with a most serene and clear sky, with moderate temperature. We had been praying for a long time that the weather might be fair, and certainly our dear Lord gave a great benediction in that line. The Mass field was as dry as could be, and also all the grounds. It was good that it was so because we had to park cars on highlands and lowlands. I never expect to see such a lineup of cars again on the premises of Gethsemani.

We began to assemble for the procession at 9:15. All the bishops, prelates, and clergy assembled in the front yard. We novices went out first as we had some singing to do; and from reports, the singing was performed very well. I, being in their midst, nearly threw them off a couple of times; but I had a few well-informed musicians on my right and left, and they held me more or less to the notes. . . . Monsignor Sheen himself spoke for a half-hour, and the governor for twenty minutes. Reverend Father spoke from ten to fifteen minutes. The whole performance from the beginning of the procession to the end of the return procession lasted two and a half hours. The bishops went out

* A town not far from the monastery.

single file with altar boys carrying very stately coats of arms poised upon ten-foot poles. It made quite a regal procession. And then the monsignori and clergy; then the Knights of Columbus in full dress uniform, followed by monks and brothers, and about 25,000 lay people. The fields were all covered with mankind. Sisters and brothers and priests and nurses galore and soldiers. . . .

The [field] altar was made chiefly by us, an expanse of about one hundred by eighty feet. It had a large canopy of white over it, and flags from the four highly-poised corner poles. There were present about thirty bishops and abbots in the sanctuary. The Cardinal presided at the throne in cappa magna, and Archbishop Floersch celebrated Mass.

Happy for us, a slight cloud filter spread over the heavens, shutting out the direct rays of Kentucky's sun. Had this cloudy effect not been present, I am afraid you would not have received this letter, for we would all have been burned to a frizzle on the spot. Even as it was, our heads and necks are still peeling because of the right smart sunburn which we all received. The Knights of Columbus looked like Indians (because of the heavy sunburn) with poised swords.

Everything went off perfectly smoothly. There did not seem to be a mistake or a hitch anywhere. It was the largest crowd I have ever seen in one spot. The cars started to stream in about 7:30 in the morning, and there seemed to be no let up to that stream into the fields and pastures. The state police took care of traffic control. . . .

In the afternoon we had Benediction of the Most Blessed Sacrament at three o'clock out in the field. A third of the crowd at least had dispersed. Our Reverend General from Rome gave the Benediction. And then along about four-thirty we donned our work clothes and started to gather up the bottles and paper, and take in the books, etc. When the eight o'clock bell sounded, we were all happy that the jubilee was over. It was really a very exhausting day. Our meridian was disturbed by the talking of people all over the house. . . . You now have all the news about the jubilee. . . .

I was glad to have talked to you all from the hospital. It was certainly like a semi-visit of the family. I am feeling very well again, although I have not taken back any weight as yet. I guess

I do not need any; I feel very well otherwise and am doing my usual round of duties. We expect quite an influx of postulants this fall; I am preparing things in advance so I can receive them with open arms when they do come.

We are passing through a very sanctifying octave, this octave of the Holy Spirit, and I do hope that He will fill your souls with light and love that you may ever fly toward the object of our eternal rejoicing. I leave you in the arms of Love until October 15.*

fr. M. Gerard, O.C.S.O.

P.S. We are having our regular visitation just now. Our community is now the largest in the Order.

I just got your letter, Ag, and the Mass for Mrs. Meath. . . . I got your A. B. Dick stencils, Syl; they will carry us for twenty-four days. . . .

Shortly after his election as Abbot of Gethsemani, Dom James appointed Father Gerard as first superior of the monastery which was to be founded later in New York state, and also named him prior of Gethsemani. His letters to his brothers and sisters gave little evidence of his added responsibilities at that time.

Trappist P.O. Ky.
December 24, 1949

Dear Eva:

"Glory be to God in high and peace on earth to men of love." There is, I am sure, great joy in heaven at this season in beholding the good will among men. We know from experience, Eva, that we feel great peace in loving God and being kind to His creatures — His children. But even this peace comes from our Lord, and relying on this truth, I feel that I am partly excused from expressing my gratitude to you, for Jesus and Mary have already reciprocated your thoughtful gift in a manner worthy of their loving hearts.

* The date of a family visit.

I speak very openly with you, but gifts touch me more tenderly now than they used to — perhaps because I cannot return them, at least in a sensible manner. I no longer look so much at the quantity of the gift as at the affection which prompted it. The more one enters into himself, the more he sees that he deserves very little recognition, and thus he admires greatly the charity of a person showing affection for him. Let us cultivate this love, Eva, that supernatural affection that is not overcome by a word or look. We may frequently feel those sacrifices which Jesus, in His little crib, asks so earnestly of us, but when we see Him, Almighty God, come down from heaven and become a poor creature like ourselves; and not only this, but also live thirty-three years in this land of exile and finally endure the awful agony of the passion and death on the cross, we can only be silent and wonder, with a will to do all for Him who has loved us so much.

I am continuing this on Christmas day amid the splendor and joy of the *Gloria in Excelsis Deo*. We had a beautiful midnight Mass at which we all communicated, and it was then, when Jesus was born in my heart, that I wished you and all a truly Merry Christmas. I feel sure, not because of my prayer but because of the love our Lord has for you, that He will give you a share in a great measure in that peace which is promised to men of good will.

I was thinking yesterday, not without a little pang of heart, of the Christmas days that we spent with Mother and Father at home. Well, we hope that those days will not only be renewed, but magnified more than our hearts can express when on the day the angel sounds the trumpet and says that time is no more, and we enter into the union of joy of Jesus and Mary, there to rest for the eternal years. Again thanks for the gift. Reverend Father gave it to the basilica fund of St. Thérèse. Pray for me, Eva. I will make a novena for you nine days preceding February 2 — unite with me.

Love,
fr. M. Gerard

Our Lady of Gethsemani
January 5, 1950
Jubilee Year of 1950

My dear Brothers and Sisters All:

It is too late to wish you a Merry Christmas, so I'll just wish you the joys of the season. The New Year is tripping merrily along its way. It finds us all at Gethsemani in the best of spirits and health. Our spirits are good because we have come to rejoice in the cross — in that which most people eschew as being one of the undesirables of life. When a person comes to rejoice in nothing quite so much as in God's holy will, one enters into a state of habitual and never-ending joy. When one goes out to satisfy self unto satiety then one puts oneself immediately in the way of sorrow. For the things of this world that we see, feel, and touch were never intended to completely satisfy the cravings of the heart of man for happiness. In fact, the things of the world as we have them now, were really intended as a means of penance, of satisfying for sin; both original and actual. God, indeed, placed Adam and Eve in a paradise of delights, but when they proved unfaithful to God's love they were driven by an angel from the garden of Eden.

Every man is out for happiness. The quest for happiness is innate in the human soul, for God made us like unto Himself with an intellect which seeks truth, and the first truth — God — contains in Himself all our delights. He has given us a will which seeks the good and ultimately the sovereign Good; here on earth to possess a good gives joy, but to possess God will constitute our eternal ecstasy. This is why the man of faith — a comtemplative soul — is as happy as possible here below in our penitential and pain-giving mortal turmoil. The soul endowed with the lynx' eyes of faith sees the beauty of God's wisdom, power, and love in everything that happens to it from within and from without. For it loves God's holy will and all that flows from His holy will in a direct or a permitted way and in this love is found the supreme joy that can be experienced by the human soul here below.

Therefore, in some wise we create our own happy New Year. And if there is in this year the real sense of happiness, then it will be for us also a personal holy year. I do hope that God will implant His grace, light and love deep into your good souls during this year of 1950 which promises to be a great year indeed in the annals of the world's history.

Since I have written you last, quite a few things have happened in our monastery — in our little Mystical Body. We sent out thirty religious to South Carolina and founded the monastery of the Immaculate Heart in one of the most picturesque spots in the scenic South. We are contemplating a fourth foundation in the rugged mountain regions of New York. The postulants have not ceased to enter since then. We are receiving three today. . . . A Chinaman is coming from Hong Kong. I don't know if he will bring his banjo with him or not. We will soon have a real orchestra here. We just received a colored man who knows how to play the saxophone. When things get a little dull around here, we can cheer up the saddened members.

We consecrated last month our new altar, recently acquired from Italy, a unique and expensive one. It was one of the longest ceremonies I've ever attended, and it is the longest ceremony in all the ecclesiastical books. A beautiful ceremony and very soul-touching, especially when one is acquainted with the Latin and symbolism of the various anointings.

I heard from each member of the family and all seem in good health. I have not been very faithful in my correspondence during the last year or so because my duties have been rather heavy during this period, and it looks as though they will continue to be so for some time to come. I have a good helper that pulls me through the quagmire when I begin to perish in the morass of it all. In the world they give time and a half for extra work, and do you think that heaven will be outdone in generosity, by the generosity of the earth's employers? It is Jesus who has hired me in His vineyard, and it is He who places tasks upon me which are beyond the capacity of my poor shoulders; but when He places His hand under me to bear me up, lest my foot stumble against a stone, then indeed things are very easy and even delectable, for He assures me, "My yoke is sweet and my burden is light." Then I am entirely freed from any temptation; the only temptation I have is drowsiness in choir. However, I am consoled by the words of the Little Flower when she was overcome by sleep. She reflected that when little children are asleep they are just as pleasing (sometimes more pleasing) to the father and mother than when they are awake.

A family visit is now in order for next spring, I understand. It seems everyone will be most free after May. I do hope that Ag's health will be improved to such a degree that she will be able to come with Sister Myron. Eva seems to be intent on going to Rome this year,* and therefore she may not be interested in our Kentucky knolls — having lifted her eyes to the Alps and beyond. Her trip to Rome will indeed be an inspiring one. She will take in Rome, Lourdes, Ol' Ireland and doubtless Fatima. . . .

Syl sent enough gloves** to supply our fathers and brothers; in fact, we are storing some away for our New York foundation. They [Syl and Madeline] will be the first benefactors.

I am going to close with a great plea placed before the Infant of the crib and His Blessed Mother that your New Year be blessed in every way; that you may enjoy soul-peace and bodily health. May this Holy Year be a personal Holy Year for you all; may it find at its close a greater union between your soul and the Heart of Jesus. In this great Heart and in the heart of His Blessed Mother may we always live in perfect bonds of family love.

Your little brother,
fr. M. Gerard

April 14, 1950

My dearest Brothers and Sisters:

Happy Easter and a joyous season to you all. May the gladsome echo of Easter Alleluias remain long in your souls.

Our Holy Week and especially our Easter Sunday were most impressive. We carried out all the ceremonies to the full, and I had the joy of singing the Passion and being assistant priest on Holy Thursday, singing a lamentation and a prophecy, be-

* Ev had arranged to join a Holy Year Pilgrimage and was to represent the family in Rome.

** Syl and Madeline's gifts to the monastery consisted of items that were practical for the monks.

sides a special piece called *in tribulatione*. All went off fairly well. We have an extraordinary professor of chant from France. He led some of the singing and thus we not only had beauty, but we had perfection as well. The professor, by the way, has been here for a couple of months, and will stay for two more months. He is teaching us the technique and intricacies of the musical art. He insists above all on the pitch. It may be that we will put out a record or two before he leaves so that others may participate in the joy of the chant.

I've heard from all the family, and they are all in good health, for which I am very grateful to our dearest Lord and ever-motherly Queen. I cannot say that our health has been good this winter. We perhaps had one of the most virulent cases of the flu that we have ever had. They had to put some name on it so they called it virus X; i.e., its power is beyond their knowledge.

I took sick on the twentieth of March, and I really was sick for one week. Some indicated that they thought I was going to die. The same day I took sick, ten or fifteen took to bed. . . . Our infirmary was overfilled, so we just slept in the dormitory; for the moment, it was turned into an infirmary. About three-fourths of the professed were in bed with it for some time. . . . The disease was malignant, infectious, and weakening. Several have not appeared at all at the community exercises even yet. Because of the use of penicillin . . . we did not have any deaths, thanks be to God, although two were sent to the hospital because of the effects [of the drug]. I was able to get up for Palm Sunday and to sing the Passion, but it is only now that I am free from all its after-effects. Brother is still giving me some orange juice as a precaution.

Ev still has her visit to Rome at heart, and I am very glad she has, for a pilgrimage to Rome is no small privilege. She will have to be our representative to the Holy Father. . . . It will certainly be an experience that will be worth all the effort that she has been putting into her preparations for the same. . . .

In regard to the family visit next May or June, I do hope that all will be able to come this year, because everything else being equal, it will be the last year you will be able to visit me at the monastery on Kentucky soil. As things stand now, it is certain that I'll be going to the new foundation. They will need various kinds of skill at the foundation. I used to have charge of all the machinery about the monastery, so I probably still could take care of trucks. I've gotten so that I can hear a confession or two; I finally got on to the formula, and they may need a confessor at the new foundation. And then, too, I've had charge of the infirmary for ten years, and it might be that I could give out a pill or two for improving the health of the sick. They'll need father masters and laundrymen and retreat masters and guest masters and servants in the refectory, and I may be able to qualify for one of these . . . in any case, it is certain that I'll be going. . . . Any time in May or June would be good [for the family to come]. I suppose that for Ev's and Sister Myron's sake it will have to be in June because their schools probably will not be out in May. It rarely gets hot in Kentucky, I mean with that good boiling temperature, until about the first of July. We will leave everything for Ev to arrange in her usual exact and suave way.

Our winter here has been a very mild one. The snow danced in the air three or four times, but there was never any to cover the ground. It has been rather cold this spring. The temperature gets down to nearly freezing at night, and even right now. It has been a rather late spring.

Reverend Father will be taking a little journey next week to ascertain for sure the site of our new foundation. I would ask you to say a little prayer that the site will be just the one that Jesus and Mary have chosen for the monastery from all eternity.

We are growing steadily. . . . Our novitiate holds at about a hundred. Our retreatants are very much on the increase. We turned away a hundred and twenty applications for retreat during Holy Week. At the present time the Mayor of Louisville is here on retreat. He is making about a two-week retreat. We have also a Protestant who is doing nearly all the work for us in the guest house. He is certainly a good soul and full of heart. I do hope that he is blessed by God in time and in eternity.

Our Kentucky knolls and valleys are beginning to brighten up with springtime splendor. Today has been about the first real spring day. . . . The temperature is warm; the early leafing trees are beginning to bud forth in bright green, and the daffodils are in full bloom. Everything reminds one that summer will close in on us soon and clothe the fields and woodlands with heart-cheering flowers and soothing, refreshing greenery. The birds have been flocking northward for some weeks. Kentucky has been enchanted with their various songs and tonalities. I walked into the cedars the other day, and I was serenaded by a thousand swallow songsters. When they flew off, they seemed to say, "We'll sing to your friends in Wisconsin and Minnesota!" I, smiling, bade them sing sweetly to you all.

As I'll be hearing from some of you and seeing you all in a month or two, I will not add any more words to this already lengthy letter. It might be well to settle on some date soon because just today I received a request for a family to come on the 16th of June.

I remembered you all during the psalter on Good Friday and in my Easter Mass. I do hope that your souls are filled with divine light and love and that your Easter joys may never wane until they are perfected in eternal bliss.

Your little brother in the Sacred Hearts of Jesus and Mary,

fr. M. Gerard, O.C.S.O.

During the Holy Year, 1950, Father Gerard's time was at a premium; nevertheless, he took time out to write his sister, who was going to Rome, and to write long messages to the whole family.

Our Lady of Gethsemani
June 22, 1950

Dear Eva:

You will soon be enroute to Rome.

It has been well said that anyone who looks at anything and fails to see God therein has not seen it. What is meant is that everything we see, from Betelgeuse to the bee, demands God as its origin and God as its present support. That is as obvious to a thinker as that every pendulum needs a fixed point from which to hang before it can swing freely.

To put the same truth in a Chestertonian cast, "Let's look at familiar things until they begin to look strange. Then, we will see them for the first time."

You are going to have time, Eva, to look at things longer than you have ever had in your life, and you must see them.

First of all, look at the ocean under the star-spangled sky — see immensity. Every effect demands a cause, and no effect can be greater than its cause. The immense ocean came from the Creator, who is immensity itself. "His strong heart stirs the ever-beating sea," says the poet. And who will question His insight? As you stare into the heavens some cloudless night on the Queen Mary, or whatever boat you are traveling on, as it pushes the Atlantic's waves to the right and left with an effortlessness that tells of man's prowess, you may suddenly feel small beneath an expanse so limitless. If you ponder on the precision of those stars that swing in orbits almost measureless to man, you will feel less than tiny. The stars have been on the wing since creation's dawn; but, although they have obeyed their Master faultlessly for eons, you, little you, tiny you, can give God more glory by a simple act of faith, a simple sigh breathed in thanksgiving for the beauty He has splashed over sky and earth and sea than the entire galaxy that makes up the Milky Way.

You, being a person like unto God by intellect and will, what you give back to Him is given freely; what the rest of creation gives Him is of necessity. You can become a very prayerful person on your journey to Rome by seeing God everywhere.

You can see Him if you but open your eyes and think as you look.

You are going to see the old country, Eva. You are going to see ancient culture. Try to see Christ down the ages. You will go to the Colosseum. You will walk through the catacombs. You will go walking on the dust that Saint Peter stirred and Saint Paul trampled upon, when there was only one power in the world, the Roman power.

You will be, as it were, neck-deep and over your head in history, philosophy, theology, sociology that came to our United States through channels of Rome and its surroundings.

These avalanches of knowledge have changed the entire face of the world. In the Roman atmosphere, you can easily see that all had its source in God, in the Incarnation. Jesus was behind it all. As you travel over Europe and visit the different monuments of antiquity, be conscious of the fact that it was the Benedictines who made Europe, and Christianity that raised up all these treasures of art, architecture, painting and sculpture. It was Jesus and Mary of Nazareth who inspired the geniuses of the days that are dead.

Eva, you will note that Europe was founded on faith. If it is crumbling today, is not the reason to be found in its faithlessness? Walk along and think and be proud of your faith and of your fathers whose bones lie beneath your feet.

I do hope that you will enjoy every moment of your trip. This is once in a lifetime, Eva, that you will pass over the ancient soil of your ancestors, that you will be greeted by those monuments which tell of things that used to be. Show your appreciation to God by making every moment of it enjoyable for all those around you and by a little uplift of it all to Him.

I hope you do not merely look, but that you see, and then you will find enjoyment in your pilgrimage — intellectual, spiritual, social, esthetic, and economic. After seven weeks in such close contact with God as He is seen in nature and in history, you cannot but come back to Davenport* a changed woman, a fit lady to instill into Joe a spirituality and a sublimation of outlook and evaluation of all about him.

My blessing upon you and upon your boat and the smallest taxi that will carry you thither and hither. And a big blessing upon your Joe who will be missing you those long days.

If you find God on this trip, you will find happiness and be closer to being a saint upon your return than you were on your departure.

Your brother who will be praying for you,
fr. M. Gerard

August 24, 1950

My dear Brothers, Sisters and All:

The feast of the Assumption has gone . . . even the feast

* The home of the Fells at that time.

of St. Bernard has passed, and I'm only now getting word to you. . . . We know that Mary is in heaven, body and soul, and that she is looking down upon us with her physical eyes. She sees us at every moment, much as a mother sees her son and daughter who are near to her. A mother often discovers beauties and loveableness in her child which actually do not exist there. We can hardly conceive how lovingly our Blessed Mother gazes upon us and how merciful is her eye and her heart. The Catholic world has always believed that the Blessed Virgin has been assumed into heaven, but the Holy Father is going to make it a dogma of faith on the 1st of November of this year. This will be another glory added to the prerogatives of our Blessed Lady.

A Christian soul, a member of the Mystical Body, ought never to be lonely — ought never to feel the pangs of ostracism, for the elite society in which it moves is not subject to whim or change. It is loved by this society and will always be loved by it, no matter what happens to it personally in the physical or moral realm. What mere men think of us or do to us is of very minor importance because factually they cannot add or detract one iota to our stature, nor can they cause me to divert one degree from the perfect fulfillment of God's holy will.

A soul goes very horizontal indeed and bedraggles the God-given wings of light and love when she puts too much weight on the opinion or the affection of men. Creatures are important, indeed, but they are only instruments in the Divine Hand which swings and sways them at will and according to the eternal designs which it has upon souls. If I am wise, I ought to use creatures as a medium to look through to the divine. They do but bring me God's holy will. Through all persons, things, and events, God is working out the divine destiny for my soul. My big role in life is to see Him loving me through all. Persons, things, and events do but manifest to me the divine action or the will of Jesus for my soul. With this enlightened outlook upon the world and all that is in it, my soul becomes beautified, resting as it does in the divine sheen of God's light and love. My life becomes happy, as happy as a life can be this side of the sight and possession of God.

By ever walking in the company of the divine Three, in the presence of my angel guardian, and arm in arm, as it were, with my dearest Mother, by living the life of faith, I will live the fullest life that is possible for man to live here below — the life of enlightened intellection and loving volition. I will be living the life of a perfect man.

My dear brothers and sisters, I almost had a distraction, I feel. However, there is not too much news. I might say that we have about 230 monks in the abbey, and everything is going on well. Our buildings are rising. Our New York foundation is in the offing! We were made very happy on the feast of the Immaculate Heart of Mary by having a man assure us that he is going out to raise funds for the building of the new monastery and for the purpose of obtaining the additional land. I'm going to ask you all to pray for this intention; pray that this monastery will be built for the glory of the Trinity and for the salvation and sanctification of souls; that it will be to the eternal praise of the Sacred Hearts of Jesus and Mary, and that it will be ever blessed by heaven's King and Queen.

Ev has, I suppose, left for the Eternal City and will be filled with European experiences when she returns home. She will do most of the writing for the coming year. Our joy will be to share with her the Holy Year's joy which will fill her soul during this pilgrimage.

I ever keep you all in my Divine Office and Holy Mass, and I hope you remember me; for I need many graces, and I need much light and strength of soul to carry on my God-given duties.

I'm going to close by commending you all to the merciful and loving hearts of Jesus and Mary, in whom I am

As ever your little brother,
fr. M. Gerard, O.C.S.O.

December 23, 1950

My dear Brothers and Sisters All:

A merry, merry Christmas to you all!

First of all, I'll have to tell you of all that has transpired since last fall. I believe I skipped my family letter last November. I was waiting to tell you of the further developings of the new foundation. . . .

As soon as Reverend Father arrived in New York, things began to develop at a rapid pace concerning our new foundation to be established at Genesee, New York. Since that time, the adjacent farm to the one which was given us has been purchased and is in our name. Mr. Chandler, who gave us the 570 acre farm . . . thought it would be well for someone to visit the site to come to a little more practical conclusion as to the temporary buildings, etc. So last November 20, three of us set sail in our car for New York. We arrived there in good season on the twenty-first, and we viewed the property.

The property . . . surpassed my expectations. It is not the most picturesque spot in the state by any means, but it is a very splendid site, and it can be developed into a very attractive site and a perfect monastery.

While we were there we stayed at a very aristocratic family's home, and we were treated by all about the place with utmost cordiality. Everyone seemed most willing to help us. . . .

We are going ahead with the preparations, and it involves a lot of negotiating, writing and buying, etc. St. Teresa of Avila became a great mystic while founding monasteries, so I suppose it is possible to unite prayer with this sort of negotiation.

Ev has sent me a number of stamps from the countries and places which she visited . . . they are all very interesting indeed. I do hope that she gets around to typing out all her experiences on her trip to Rome. It will be most interesting reading for the long winter months. Personally, however, I don't find much difficulty in keeping occupied. My chief trouble is the shortness of the hours in the day. I find that if I had about two or three hours more each day, I would finish my work as I had planned it, especially at this Christmas season, when one has a thousand letters each day to wade through. They are not all sent to me, however. . . .

Everything is well here in the monastery. We have gone beyond the 250 mark . . . we are stretching out now for the 300. Some thirty have been sleeping out in a tent during the zero weather. It was so cold in those tents that when they woke up in the morning, they found their shoes frozen to the floor. Our retreat master, a seasoned old Dominican, called our outside tent "Skid Row." Our buildings are rearing, although it has been too cold for some time to work on them; but this has not been without good results, for in the meantime they have made some altars for the new foundation.

Tomorrow is Christmas Eve, and everything is beginning to shape around into the loveliness which that day suggests. . . . Our Christmas this year will be the merriest that has ever been had in Gethsemani, according to the old slogan . . . : "The more the merrier. . . ." Hence, since we have never had so many at Gethsemani before, neither will there be any end to our joy this Christmas. Each one will add joy to the other. . . .

This Christmas will be the most grace-full Christmas that we ever had. It will be more grace-full than the first Christmas would have been had we sung with the angels on the Judean hills and gone down with the shepherds to kneel between Joseph and Mary adoring the Divine Babe. Because grace was more abundantly released when Jesus died on Calvary's height, and that grace is being applied to our souls through the holy sacrifice of the Mass, from which the sacraments flow as so many channels carrying us the grace which was bought for us on Calvary and applied through the Mass.

St. Bernard says that it is not said that Jesus *was* born in Bethlehem of Juda, but that He *is born*. There will be Masses offered in Bethlehem tomorrow, and Jesus will be as truly present in those Masses as He was when He appeared as a little Babe in the crib two thousand years ago. When I enter into church tomorrow I can kneel and adore the same divine Babe that nestled in the straw before the ecstatic gaze of Joseph and Mary. . . . He is there with His body and blood, soul and divinity; He is there as the all-adorable Babe. He is He through whom we have all; in whom we have all; from whom we have all. He is indeed the God of love.

Our attitude during these hours ought to be that of adoring awe. God has so loved the world as to give His only begotten Son! If Jesus did not love us, He would not lie there in the crib. The very sight of Jesus in the crib ought to open up vast vistas of light concerning God's love for us. It ought to take away all fear and all doubt. It ought to be the great overpowering motive that throws us into the arms of our all-powerful and all-loving Father. If at any time, surely during this Christmas season, love should be our life.

Just to gaze upon the new flash of lovableness that has come over the countenance of our dearest Mother at the first moment of her divine maternity is enough to draw our hearts irresistibly to her and cause us to adhere to her in an embrace of confident love. Besides the great manifestation of God's love to us, Christmas reveals to us, as never before, the lovable and maternal affection of Mary for her children. You can style her mother as never before, now; being the Mother of the physical Jesus, she is Mother of the mystical Christ, in whom we are.

I do ask you all to pray for our intentions during the coming few months, because they will be months which will require much light and much strength; and we can only obtain that from the Holy Ghost, the sweet Spirit of Jesus.

I will be remembering you all in my three Christmas Masses tomorrow; in fact, two of them are for the intentions of Sister Myron. . . . All will be included. I will ask the little Jesus to bestow upon you all the plenitude of His blessing and to grant you all the graces that your souls can contain, and give you all the physical aids in good health and accomplishments according to His divine will.

So again, a peaceful, joyful, and a merry Christmas to all my near and dear ones.

In the Sacred Hearts of the little
King and the sweetest of Queens,
Your little brother,

fr. M. Gerard, O.C.S.O.

III

PIONEERING IN A NEW MONASTERY AT PIFFARD, NEW YORK

FATHER GERARD was soon to leave for New York as superior of the new foundation there. The family asked to spend a day with him to commemorate his twenty-fifth year at the Kentucky monastery.

It was the Porter Chandler family of Genesee, New York, who gave the Kentucky Trappists the property on which to build the first Cistercian abbey in the Empire State. Bishop James E. Kearney invited the monks to make a foundation in his diocese. After that, all the Trappists needed was willing hands to help build a chapel and quarters for the monks.

When Father Gerard's brother, Sylvester, heard that the monks would soon be in Piffard, New York, the site of the new monastery, he and his wife made ready to spend a month there to help them in whatever way they could.

From Kentucky, Father Gerard wrote notes of welcome to Syl and Madeline, expressing his great joy that they were willing to help.

Trappist, Ky.
March 1, 1951

Dear Syl and Madeline:

I received your good letter and read it amid joyful tears.

The situation is this: the renter is moving off today from one of our farms. The other two houses will be occupied for a year.

This one house is now vacant. We had the water shut off and furnace closed. There may be a necessity of altering the insurance because of unoccupancy.

Things are beginning to arrive in Piffard, New York, from various places and from donors. It would be most desirable that you come as soon as you reasonably can.

You can live in Porter Chandler's (the lawyer who gave us a 570-acre farm) house until the other house can be cleaned. Eight children just moved out so I suppose it means cleaning. A couple of brothers will haul a load of things up and could help with the cleaning; then you could move on the Chandler farm.

Do you have much furniture to take? Would you put all in a trailer behind your car? It might be possible for me to meet you at Cleveland [Ohio], and go up with you to get you organized a bit. . . .

A thought comes just now. If you really got zealous you might sound out some truck company (a big one) or get several together and have them donate a truck, put your stuff in, let Madeline drive your car behind. Splendid! Sister Myron says that you do a good deed toward a man when you separate him from his money, especially if it be for Christ the King.

All the New Yorkers are so very helpful; each vies with the other in doing things for us.

A crew of brothers will be going up after Easter to prepare.

We will take a load of stuff up in a week or two, depending on the weather.

I'll be expecting to hear from you soon.

Blessings upon you both.
In Jesus and Mary,

fr. M. Gerard, O.C.S.O.

Our Lady of Gethsemani
April 2, 1951

Dear Syl and Madeline, Pioneers and Guardians of Christ the King and beloved Children of Our Lady of the Genesee,*

Welcome, to the Genesee Valley and to the little village of Piffard. It was a delight to hear your voice last night coming from Admiral Chanler's "Sweetbriar Farm." I did not believe that you would arrive so early; I'm glad that you did because of Porter Chandler.

I have no anxiety but that you will receive a very warm welcome into the Chanler and Chandler circles. They are wonderful people with a good tint of English manners. Mrs. Admiral Chanler is a Du Pont. . . .

We shall be arriving in the afternoon of Thursday. I fear our Mass in Cleveland will be at a later hour than I had planned, and that will delay our arrival at Piffard—we'll probably get there around three p.m.

We are planning on having Mass the next morning—the Feast of St. Benedict—in the Piffard church. Do you know how to sing the ordinary sung parts of the Mass? If not, we shall either get Mrs. Clowser—if she knows how—or we will sing it ourselves. But sing it we will. Our general plan is to stay at Porter's house with you for a few days, and then we shall see from there on.

I cannot tell you, Syl and Madeline, how appreciative I am of this grand overture on your part towards Christ the King and Our Lady of the Genesee. It is an admirable thing for a religious to devote his entire life to the service of the Saviour and souls, but it seems that there is a special sign of rare love in the act which you are performing at this time. St. Bernard says that for a man to be a little generous and to rise a little higher in his spiritual endeavors and ideals is a rare thing upon earth. This is just what you have done.

Jesus is divine, and He never forgets; and what you are doing at Our Lady of the Genesee will be recorded by Him in His

* Syl and Madeline are now in Piffard, where this letter is addressed.

eternal memory. It will have its kingly and lavish reward, especially as He sees that you are doing it for Mary, Queen of the Angels, Queen of the Saints, Queen of the Genesee.

I do hope that your lives will go on in a peaceful, loving, and God-blessed way. Some crosses there must be, for we are still in earth's exile; and it is only by suffering that our love for Jesus and Our Lady can be purified and made entirely unselfish.

We shall join you in a few days in this grand work for the furthering of God's glory in building a monastery to the honor and praise of Christ the King, to the honor of Mary, unto the salvation of souls.

I do hope that some day the Genesee Valley will resound with the multitudinous voices of those who love God and who are bent on praising His holy name. May saints tread the banks of the Genesee, and may God be eternally loved and blessed because of the Monastery of Christ the King — because of the house of prayer, Our Lady of the Genesee.

Every blessing be yours and may your souls ever rest under the Savior's benediction — under the Motherly protection of Mary — and may you ever abide in the joys of Resurrection until the dawn of the eternal happy Easter.

Your little brother in the love and service
of the King and Queen of heaven,
fr. M. Gerard

Syl and Madeline arrived early in Piffard to help prepare for the coming of the monks and brothers. They knew Father Gerard was a diabetic and would likely forget about his diet during the pioneering days. So Madeline prepared his diet and cooked for the religious during the first days of the foundation. Good neighbors helped to supply food and other necessities, graciously welcoming the monks to their new home.

The first Trappists lived for a few weeks at Westerly, Chandler's summer residence nearby. The pastor of St. Raphael's Church, Father Charles Reynolds, invited the monks to use the church in Piffard for their services. Later the monks moved to the old Harris farm, which they named Bethlehem Place. They soon cleared the residence of chickens and began to build their monastery from "scratch."

Volunteer workers soon arrived from Rochester, thirty miles north of the monastery, and from nearby villages, to help the monks build and to remodel farm buildings. A friend sent thousands of rose plants which Father Gerard wanted planted without delay because roses would beautify their new home.

Father Gerard made a few trips back to Kentucky before everything was settled. From there he wrote Madeline and Syl, asking them to stay on at Piffard until he returned there.

Our Lady of Gethsemani
April 17, 1951

Dear Syl and Madeline:

I've been waiting to sit down and have a little talk with you. I've been thinking of and praying for you during these days. You've been sort of pressed between difficulties for some time — I hope that they are being ironed out somewhat.

I don't know what I would have done without you; you have been an immense help to our first steps in founding Our Lady of the Genesee. What you have done will go down on the annals of the monastery and will be stowed away in the archives of the monastery for posterity to admire and praise. You'll be intimately associated with the graces bestowed upon those who undertake to do something to further the kingdom of God — to further the reign of love upon the earth. . . .

Incidentally, Reverend Father saw Porter and Bibo (Mrs. Chandler) in New York the other day, and they spoke very highly of you. Bibo said that she thought Madeline was a very lovely character and that everybody in Piffard liked her — this is one certain sign that you are very welcome in her home. . . .

I think everything will work out very harmoniously that way; especially when we get out of the house you will not feel the pressure. One could hardly ask for a better all-around man than Porter Chandler — he is simply excellent. Mrs. Chandler, too, is a very lovable lady. . . .

I wonder if you could stay until I get there again. Unless we hear a definite word from France that the Visitor will be here very soon, I shall come up again to New York next Saturday or Sunday (April 21 and 22). If that would not be too late a date for you to start back to Minneapolis, I would very much like you to stay so that I could have a few words with you and get the general layout of what is going on when I arrive.

The three brothers will start up early Friday morning: Brothers Hugh, Martin and Barnabas . . . they should arrive Saturday at an early hour. They will pick up some machinery in Cincinnati.

I hope that you have found a good board for the attic — I would get a very light one and rather inexpensive, although it should have some properties of insulation. I hope you found some bottled gas. With regard to the cardboard, it might be well to contact Sam Lipani; he might be able to direct you to some place in Rochester where you might make a good deal.

Father Ambrose was speaking about plowing a furrow and putting the roses in and then letting the furrow fall back . . . you would still have your sod, wouldn't you? Anyway, I suppose as long as the directions are there you'll be able to figure out better than I know. I still think that perhaps a small load of that black soil, which James Johnson could tell you about, might be a good kind of soil to put around the roses.

If I come up Saturday or Sunday, I'll take a tabernacle with me so we can reserve the Blessed Sacrament at Nazareth Place.

I think that is about all for the moment — all goes well here. It is rather cold and wet, a very late spring in Kentucky.

With every good blessing upon you and Madeline, I close,

In the Sacred Hearts of Jesus and Mary,

fr. M. Gerard

Father Gerard was overjoyed when he heard that Syl and Madeline had offered their services to the new monastery as long as they were needed. Syl had left the Internal Revenue Department to open a tax office in Minneapolis. He now closed the office and he and his wife gave their services to the new monas-

tery at Piffard, N. Y. Gerard never tired of expressing his thanks for this gesture of genuine charity.

Our Lady of Gethsemani
May 2, 1951

Dear Syl and Madeline:

I am glad to have word from you after your arrival in Minneapolis. I have been delighted with all the good things you've been doing for me at Piffard, where through my little Trappist brothers, I'm trying to establish a house of praise and adoration to the honor and glory of my Father.

The love which has prompted you to offer your lives for the cause is a great joy to me and to my Mother [Mary]. She sees more of me in you now than she saw before because of this increase in love. . . .

My little Trappist brothers were delighted at having you with them at the Chandler home, and their gratitude to you will be eternal. You will ever have a large share in their prayers and sacrifices. . . .

It'll be a consolation to you for me to tell you that you will ever abide in my love and care, and my choicest blessings will descend upon the souls of my Madeline and Sylvester.

I shall be waiting for you at Bethlehem Place, and I'm sure our mutual love will ever increase. I cannot be unfaithful. . . . Be faithful, and your eternity will be one that the angels will marvel at.

In your loving Saviour, Jesus, and in your Mother Mary,
fr. M. Gerard

Our Lady of Gethsemani
May 3, 1951

Dear Syl and Madeline,

I received Madeline's card today. I must tell you that I cannot find the address of that priest to whom you told me to send the cheese so I'm sending it to you today, and you can forward it to him.

We are having our visitation just now, and I don't know how soon I'll be able to get back to New York. Pray for me during these days, for much depends on the decision of the Visitor concerning the foundation. The Holy Ghost works during these days, and I hope that Jesus will so arrange that we'll have just the community that He chose from all eternity. I hope to get ten lay brother novices.

I'll keep you especially in my Mass and Offices that everything goes well with you. Kindly keep me informed as to your plans.

With every good wish and blessing upon you,

I close in the Sacred Hearts of Jesus and Mary,

fr. M. Gerard

Our Lady of Gethsemani
May 15, 1951

Dear Syl and Madeline:

This is perhaps the last word I shall be penning you from Kentucky as I shall be in New York soon myself.

I just want to write you my plans. I shall be taking a load of novices tomorrow, the sixteenth, and I shall be back here next Saturday, the nineteenth, to take another load the following Wednesday, the twenty-third. We will have to stay at Porter's house because we don't have enough bunks at Bethlehem Place. They will go up on the truck which will leave next Monday or Tuesday.

Everything else is going quite well, in fact, very fast. When I arrive next Thursday, we will have a meeting with Sam Lipani, Paul Eschbaugh, Mr. Herbert,* etc. Mr. Cooney is helping them. Mr. Stanton from Cleveland is sending ten men as laborers the first of June. So the buildings will go up quickly once we get started. We could build five monasteries, I am convinced, if it is God's will to have that number. If we have courage

* A few of the many devoted benefactors of the monastery.

and confidence just to do our part, we will see marvels of divine grace and divine magnificence.

I do hope that you will have a safe journey back to New York — back home. I shall be with you and rejoice in the grace of the home life very soon.

In the peace of the Holy Ghost
and the love of Jesus and Mary,
fr. M. Gerard

Before leaving Kentucky, Gerard wrote home, acknowledging the great good that had come to him while at Gethsemani.

May 22, 1951

My dear Brothers and Sisters,

I am sitting down this afternoon to pen these words in my last letter from Kentucky. I have written you often from this hallowed spot, and I am beginning to feel the nearness of my departure.

I was called at a comparatively early age to enter this abbey at Gethsemani and to fight in this holy garden the battle of the Lord. I have battled, indeed, but I have not fought perfectly. I want to thank Jesus, Mary, and the whole heavenly court for all the good that has come to my soul in this abbey, and I want to thank you for your prayers which helped me to persevere in this calling.

The time has now come by God's holy will to depart to other fields of service and in other capacities of office. I shall be leaving for New York on Friday, May twenty-fifth, and I will not return to Gethsemani, at least not frequently or soon. So any letters that you write after that date should be addressed to me at Our Lady of the Genesee, Piffard, New York.

I have known that I would be going for some time. Reverend Father Abbot James acquainted me with this appointment to New York on August twenty-second, the feast of the Immaculate Heart of Mary, during the octave of St. Bernard, 1949. He told me that I would act as prior until I left. So last Sunday he appointed a new prior, but I shall remain in office until I leave.

I shall take a car full of novices with me to New York Friday morning. Then we shall have nineteen religious up there when we arrive. We are beginning to shape up into a regularly established monastery. We hope to get the buildings up soon so we can take the rest of the community up. I think I shall be happy in a natural way in New York. We have everything we have here at Gethsemani and when our buildings are completed we shall have more than here. The climate is much more conducive to Trappist life. Our farm will be better. We will have better surroundings and if our Lord, as I hope He will, deigns to please us and if our Lady kindly smiles upon us we ought to go on and flourish in New York. I do hope that everything that will be done there will be done in the honor and glory of the Trinity, the Father, the Son, and the Holy Ghost, to the praise of Christ the King and to the good pleasure of Our Lady of the Genesee, for the salvation and sanctification of souls. I do not have any more to say on my departure except that I raise my hand over you all and give you my last blessing from Kentucky soil.

May your souls ever live in the light and love and peace of the Holy Ghost and may we all be gathered together some day in the eternal realm, in the great divine family of God's loving children.

With every blessing upon you,

In the Sacred Hearts of Jesus and Mary,
fr. M. Gerard

His last note before leaving Kentucky was addressed to Mother Gethsemani, his home for more than a quarter of a century.

I loved your turrets and towers and spires, pointed up to eternal goals and everlasting attainments. I loved your basilica with its great marble altar and its magnificent tabernacle — the home of heaven's eternal King.

I viewed with great joy your serried ranks of cowled characters, chanting lovingly and sweetly to the august Three, raising their voices in praise to the King of Ages, and in dulcet tones, hymning Mary, the lovely Lady of the eternal realms, and the Queen of May.

I walked with soothed soul and in pensive mood amid the tombs of those I loved, now resting in your silver-crested cemetery.

I experienced many inspirations and felt shoals of love inundate my soul as I passed with measured tread through your time-worn cloisters. I passed for the last time through your gardens, and sweet memories pressed in upon my soul. I recall all the love that was put into the work and labor as a novice down the cabbage and celery rows. I recall, without regret, the many drops of perspiration that flowed down my brow as I looked forward with eager hope to the salvation and sanctification of my soul. . . .

I walked with our Lady down the stately paths of Kentucky knolls. I talked with her and asked her to bless the monks, my friends, my brothers, whom I left behind. I asked her to spread her mantle over the confines of Gethsemani that she might ever mother those who live there and those who have died on its battlefields of prayer.

I sat with great delight in the chapter room and listened to the teaching of three abbots. All were loved, all were revered, but none more than the venerable abbot who now graces the abbatial throne. I have smarted under the lash of paternal correction, but it has built up my soul and has shown me how to glue my will to the divine will in a way that perhaps nothing else could have done. God bless the holy abbots who have corrected me in mercy and brought much grace to my soul. May their names ever be in benediction, and may they be grace-laden in eternity.

I have enjoyed the long evening hours before the tabernacle of the King of Love. I could almost see Him passing out His grace and His paternal benediction to all the brothers in white and in brown. I could all but behold the angels that passed to and fro amid the songs of praise, and often have I asked for the eternal blessing of each one of my brothers.

Mother Gethsemani, I am leaving now, and I ask that you bless all those who have lived and have gone forth and who have died on this blessed soil amid the knolls of dear old Kentucky. . . .

fr. M. Gerard, O.C.S.O.

The Chandler property, about a mile away from Piffard, was an ideal spot for a new monastery. On the highest point of the land Father Gerard planted a simple wooden cross on which was inscribed: "Foundation of the monastery of Blessed Mary of the Genesee, May 26, 1951. May God be glorified in all things. Serve the Lord with gladness."

No one was more grateful for financial assistance when starting a new venture than Father Gerard, who wrote to Ev, December 31, 1951, to thank her for remembering the new monastery, at Christmas.

What a Christmas gift, and how much we needed it! A hundred dollars! If one out of every thirteen hundred people in New York state alone would give us as much as you have given us, we would build the most beautiful monastery that has ever been seen between the two oceans.

Your names will go down and be cemented into our foundation, and the monks that pray here long years after we have departed will be praying for you; or, as I hope, be adding new praise to your name, while you rejoice in everlasting bliss.

I am so glad that you sent Sister Myron the check [for her train fare]. Perhaps sometime next June will be a grand [time to come], just when the New York roses are fairest and the songs of the birds are sweetest, and the Piffardians are in their best mood. Then we will be very happy to welcome you into this valley of Mary's smile, which is paralleled by very few, if any, of New York's pleasant places.

Syl and Madeline spent the best Christmas they ever spent, they said, in their little cracker box home. . . .

All blessings be yours. . . . Smile and sing, to Christ the King, with Mary.

fr. M. Gerard, O.C.S.O.

Pioneering at the new monastery was a challenging experience, which Gerard enjoyed to the full, according to his letters.

Our Lady of the Genesee
January 25, 1952
Conversion of Saint Paul

My dear Brothers and Sisters:

Christmas season is not yet over; perhaps that is a joyful announcement to you. I am getting well under the wire of Yuletide. I am sitting here away off in New York placidly watching the gently falling snow. Perhaps I am somewhat beforetime in giving you an account of a New York winter, because I remember mother's old saying: "Have half your feed and half your hay on Candlemas Day." It may be I can give you a better account next Easter of a New York winter; however, up until now we have had a very mild winter, I would say. It started early, however, about the first of November, but we hardly had a frost up until that time, and a more glorious fall one could scarcely dream of. The charm and beauty of this Valley of Mary's Smile conjoined with the balmy atmosphere made it a paradisiacal abode during the autumnal months.

The temperature has scarcely dropped below zero, except one day when it went down to six below. This morning it crept to eight or ten above. Perhaps when the wind swerves around and comes down Buffalo way, and we partake of the sweeping gust of the windy city, it will be different. . . .

I have had a pair of ski shoes on this winter for the first time in twenty-five years. It reminded me of the many times that Oscar Dedrickson, Joseph Gilstead* and I skipped over the

* Two of Gerard's old classmates.

Viking hills and through the snow-filled valleys. I am reminded here that Bill made me my first pair of skiis, and a right good job he did on them.

We do not have many visitors in the winter time although people do bring us things from time to time. Our next door neighbor gave us two tons of hay, and shortly after one of his cows presented him with twin calves. He feels like giving a couple of more tons to the monastery. We have a nice herd of cows, about fifteen, with about twenty calves and a few yearlings.

We are taking off thorn apple trees from the farm during the winter. They are infernal pests in this section of the country. Some of our pastures are completely overrun by them. We have 140 acres of wheat in, and we plowed all winter. We are going to put in three hundred acres of assorted seed in the spring. Our heads are full of propositions for the new season. Each one of us is worse than the other when it comes to farm plans. We have no horses, and I don't believe we will get any. We have two tractors and a caterpillar. We might have to get a little "C" tractor in the spring.

Our buildings are going up. We keep on building and buying materials even though we don't have a cent. We are daily expecting and/or hoping for the arrival of a millionaire who wants to unburden himself of his income tax worries.

I am writing this letter on the Feast of the conversion of Saint Paul . . . [who wrote] "In God we live, we move, and are." Change the word *God* to *Love* and what a beautiful sentence we have: "In Love we live, we move, and are." Who is this Love? It is the Three Persons: Father, Son, and Holy Ghost, who are always with us and who possess our soul as their very own. I am always with the Father, Son and Holy Ghost, and they are ever present to me. How beautiful is life when lived in all its reality. When we realize that we are never out of converse with or out of the presence of the august and adorable Three.

I do hope this year of 1952 will go on in love, that your souls might ever near the Divine and become dear to Him, who has come down upon earth to seek us and to die for us and to offer Himself anew daily at Mass. May the year consist of a mutual smile between you and Jesus. If you ever smile at Jesus in all that He wills you to do or sends to you, then a smile will ever play upon His adorable countenance; and the smile of Jesus means life everlasting and sainthood.

So smile and sing to Christ the King through Mary.

Your loving brother,
fr. M. Gerard

September 20, 1952

My dear Brothers and Sisters All:

Here in the Valley of the Genesee we are just as good as being in eternity because here we can say with the angel of the Apocalypse: "Time is no more." Syl feels that he, too, has entered into eternal bliss; for with him, like with the angels, time is nearly obliterated. Madeline has not yet passed completely into eternity, but she lives in time only between visits. She entertains people of every age, race, and clime. She had a negro party the other day with party hats and all.

I enjoyed Ev's round-about letter. I always admired Ev's beautiful thoughts, but now that she has suggested that the family buy the altar candlesticks, I am persuaded that she is inspired. . . .

Syl is paying for all the building material and buying cows, etc., by selling our bread. He really has the knack and monopoly on the selling world. I have heard of people buying their way into heaven, but Syl is selling his way in. . . .

We will certainly have a splendid place by next summer when you all come for a visit. We plan to have the Bishop out on the twenty-sixth of October, when we will have a little house-warming and blessing.

We have had a very hot and dry summer — extraordinarily so. One old man said that he never saw the like since the Crogan boys were hung. Our wheat was fairly good. We got three thousand bushels. Our oats were poor . . . only three thousand bushels off two hundred acres.

I went out yesterday and bought three of the finest cows in New York. I did not have a cent in my pocket. But I managed to trade in some of our grade cows for them. . . . Syl went to a sale and bought a silage feeder without buying any cows to feed and without having any silage to put into the feeder.

We are getting along very nicely. . . . I hope that by the time you get here next summer, the sun will be shining upon our little monastery full sheen. People are very appreciative of having a religious house here, and they show their appreciation in many and varied ways. Frater Dennis* seems to be working miracles, according to many reports. Father Cirrincione reads his letters on the air every night. A nearby parish where a mission was held had a sermon on Frater Dennis. We already have many, many friends, and we are beginning to extend out to Buffalo and Syracuse. However, we are expecting all good things from our Lord and our Lady. Any friend that might come to us is sent and must be sent by them, and any aid that we might receive is a result of their loving thought of us. We know that we cannot fail, having the King and the Queen on our side. We cannot fail financially because they will take care of their monastery. We cannot fail in the apostolate because prayer and sacrifice are infallible in obtaining their end. Just as Jesus cannot fail, neither can a life of prayer and sacrifice which is His life, fail.

This is the month of the Little Flower, and she speaks to us from heaven now as she would speak to us upon earth. "If you wish to become a saint (and saints we must be), then have but one intention: to please Jesus in everything." We must get love into our lives, and love means doing the will of the Beloved. All for Jesus, all from Jesus; all for Love, all from Love.

I do hope that Our Lady of the Genesee bestows a great blessing upon you all and that your lives may be peaceful, happy and loving; that you ever draw nearer to the Sacred Heart by desire and fidelity to His grace. There is only one road to happiness here below and that is the way of goodness and conformity of our will to God's will. You always have a remembrance at Our Lady of the Genesee.

All for Jesus, through Mary, with a smile.

Your little brother,
fr. M. Gerard, O.C.S.O.

---

* The first monk to die at the monastery.

April 4, 1953

Dear Brothers and Sisters All,

We have just come out of a very beautiful and grace-laden Holy Week. In the bursting light of Easter's dawn, I want to wish you all a most joyous and soul-felt happy Easter. The liturgy of Lent and the last three days of Holy Week are most apt for preparing one's soul for the inrushes of divine love. . . .

We have fifty in our community, and we were able to carry out the ceremonies to the full. We have a beautiful little church with a very splendid altar imported from Italy, which will be consecrated on the thirtieth of May. We had about thirty retreatants here these last days — the largest number we have ever had in our short life as a monastery.

We had a very mild winter with very little snow and very little cold weather. Spring is now dawning upon us, and the robins are singing and flitting about. Myriads of geese are dotting the skies.

Syl and Madeline are defending the northern front and entertaining our lady guests with true Christian charity and graciousness. Syl has been fencing some two hundred acres as an initial cattle ranch of Our Lady of the Genesee. He was stretching a mile fence the other day. He was showing the brothers just how to do it when all the posts came out! So he went home that night with great chagrin. But the next day he told them all to stand aside, and he performed the feat himself, unto the great admiration of all the brothers. We have seventy-five head of cattle to go into these extraordinary pastures. . . . The choir religious have been busy clearing the plots of thorn-apple trees before the advent of the . . . herds. Our fencing . . .[five or six miles of it] is one of our big works this spring. . . .

We are now hauling stones for our future building . . . hauling from Warsaw, a village twenty miles away. We bought $3,000 worth of stone for $200. . . .

It seems that we will have no dearth of vocations in this fertile valley. We have twenty novices now, and several are entering when school is out. We are making records with regard to a growing foundation. We are, of course, right in the midst of Catholicism and in the most populous part of the United States;

and we have the smile of our Lady, also, added to the good graces of Jesus, Saviour and King. Then, too, we have a saint, and possibly two,* who have already gone to heaven to plead our cause in the eternal courts. . . .

We are expecting our Father Immediate from France next Sunday, and he may raise our monastery to the dignity of an abbey.** Please pray that this might be the case if it be for the greater honor and glory of God.

As I will be seeing you in the not-too-distant future, I will leave you all, in the meantime, under the sheen of Mary's maternal love and under the omnipotent, omniscient, and all-loving eye of our dearest heavenly Father.

Every best blessing upon you all, in the realm of health and grace.

All for Jesus, through Mary, with a smile.

fr. M. Gerard, O.C.S.O.

The monastery became an abbey on September 13, 1953. The next step was to elect an abbot, a father for the new abbey. On October 13, a little note came to the family announcing the results of the election:

This morning at eight o'clock we sang our solemn Mass of the Holy Ghost, invoking His light upon the election of the new abbot. All assembled in chapter after the Mass, and with all the doors of the monastery tightly barred, as the Rule prescribes, we started balloting. I am hastening to give you the newest tidings of the election, and with these words go my heartiest blessing.

fr. M. Gerard, Abbot-elect

The blessing of the newly elected abbot was set for November ninth in the Cathedral at Rochester, when the pontifical insignia of his office — miter, pectoral cross, crosier, and ring —

* Father Gerard here refers to Frater Dennis and Father Simon, both deceased.

** A new monastery does not become an abbey until it is officially approved.

were given to Abbot Gerard. Bishop James E. Kearney blessed the abbot of the monastery in the presence of abbots, priests, Father Gerard's brothers and sisters, religious, other relatives, and lay people. Choir monks in their white robes and brothers in brown habits with shaved heads and beards, all from Our Lady of the Genesee Abbey, attended the first ceremony of its kind in the cathedral.

In a letter to his brothers and sisters, Father Gerard gave his own reaction to the event a few months later.

Our Lady of the Genesee
January 15, 1954

Dear Brothers and Sisters:

I just finished singing a pontifical High Mass, and it was beautiful beyond compare. It might have been a little hard to prepare oneself for the position of an abbot, but it was worthwhile just to sing one pontifical Mass. Everything is so quiet and so calm and there is such a long time between prayers that one can really suck all the honey out of those beautiful words which the Church has put on our lips in the Holy Sacrifice of the Mass.

I want to extend to you all, my dear sisters and brothers, a heart-sprung wish and prayer for all the graces which can befit your souls during this beautiful Marian Year which we joyfully have begun. I wish you all material prosperity, as much as is in conformity with God's holy will, and the holy wishes of Mary. . . .

We can hope for great things during this Marian Year. We can expect things which are beyond all hope and expectation because it is Mary's year, and that means much and very much because Mary is the mother of God and the mother of men. Think what she will do for her children in this year consecrated to her maternal heart, to her Immaculate Conception.

It has been a very eventful year, this past year of 1953. It saw the opening of our monastery on May thirtieth, and the advent of many young men to swell our ranks so that we come very near the number of seventy in our community. Then, on September thirteenth we saw the raising of our monastery to the dignity of an abbey and the election of the new abbot. It is a great event and a great step in the life of a superior, a Cistercian monk, to be raised to the dignity of an abbot. It means an entire metamorphosis of life. He is raised from the status of child to father, from a religious in the ordinary rank and file to the dignity of a prelate; and he is given a burden that is beyond the understanding of man. He is given charge of souls, and he is made responsible for the very salvation and sanctification of all those who enter the monastery. But, also, grace is added to his being, and God enlarges his heart so that he is strong and capable enough to measure up to all his obligations. He is given the added light to see clearly all that he must do, and how he may perfectly fulfill God's will in himself, in his monastery, and in his spiritual children.

God had given me, as it were, a presage of what was going to befall me in 1953. At the time that I entered Gethsemani, I asked the Abbot if there was something to sign whereby I could never be made abbot. But he told me to leave that in the hands of Almighty God, and so I did. Again, when I was a novice, the father master said, "Why, you don't know but some day you will be sitting here where I am, as father master." And so I was. Again he said, after he had been changed from the prior position, "You are the future prior." And so I was made prior. Then there was an abbot who has now gone to heaven who said, "Someday you will be abbot." And so here it is, and God's will be done.

There are two sentiments in the heart of every abbot. They are fear and joy. It is a real joy to be made the father of a large family and to have spiritual sons such as I have at Our Lady of the Genesee. They are full of affection, full of obedience, full of goodness, God-given goodness. It warms one's soul no end to feel that they depend upon me and are full of prayer and full of divine love.

. . . No Christmas that I have ever spent in my life was so full of joy and so full of the spirit of God's goodness and kindness and paternity and jubilation as the Christmases that I have spent here at Our Lady of the Genesee. . . . These are joys which are given to a man who has to bear heavy burdens indeed.

. . . I might as well tell the truth about it. It's a real joy to me. And the big joy results from my relations with my spiritual children, whom I love with my whole heart.

I am happy for your sake, for my family's sake, because I believe it was a real joy to you to come here and be present at the abbatial blessing and to feel that all those prayers that the good bishop said were going to be realized in the soul of your little brother who is the last and the least of the family. If all these prayers will be realized in him, how much more will your own souls be blessed this year by Mary, Queen of Pontiffs, because of your older age and your older growth in holiness.

It was very sweet to have the family here on that grace-laden day of the abbatial blessing. I did not have many words with any of you, but words were not necessary on that day because our hearts spoke intuitively.

It was without a doubt the happiest day of my life. . . .

I would like to have spoken with Lottie* and some of my cousins and nieces, but the occasion did not allow it.

The spirit of all the people around was very beautiful and soul-satisfying. They seemed to be just as happy as if I belonged to their own family. In fact, one, when she was receiving her blessing, looked up at me and said, "I'm just as happy as if you were my own brother." And there were several in the cathedral at Rochester who were in tears because of joy and happiness.

I have received letters from all, saying how they rejoiced over the blessing. It was a day of joy also for our community because they have the real spirit of sons, and they rejoice over the fact that they were receiving a full-fledged father on that day. In fine, it was a day whose effects and graces will run up into the eternal years, and I hope that we will rejoice in eternity over this feast day that we have spent on earth. It seems almost as a dream now. Everything that transpired was so unexpected, as it were, and so full of graces, and seemed to come directly from heaven, that it was wonderful, admirable, astonishing.

I don't see any feast days ahead. It will be 1960 before I celebrate my silver jubilee as a priest.

Syl and Madeline are reigning as king and queen over the north section of the monastery, and over the guest department, and in the name of you all I want to thank them for the grand family reunion dinner while you were here. It was the best dinner that I ever sat down to. I think Madeline will be chosen

* Gerard's godmother.

Queen of the Cooks in heaven, and perhaps queen of a lot of other realms, too. . . .

Everything is going on very well here at the monastery. We had two pontifical High Masses on Christmas and then one on the two following feasts, St. Stephen and St. John. We had our first ordination the other day, too, and a solemn profession on the feast of St. Stephen. We have quite a few postulants arriving; we'll have easily seventy by the beginning of next summer.

We are putting up a barn next spring. This is our big project right now: where to put it and what kind of a barn to build. We now have 114 head of cattle . . . and we hope to go into a good herd of Holsteins.

I see that this letter is getting rather long, so I'm going to wish you all the happiness and joy and grace of a beautiful Marian Year — this year. Don't forget our dearest Mother [Mary]. I will speak to you about her in the next letter but in the meantime, remember that you can expect extraordinary things this year. Ask her for great things, above all, spiritual things — not so much material — leave that to her maternal hands. But ask her to bestow some grace upon you, some grace that you don't even think of asking for, and that will be best, to leave all in her motherly hands. She knows how to take care of her children. Every best blessing upon you all, my dear brothers and sisters. Don't forget to keep me in your prayers that I might discharge my responsibility in a way that is pleasing to Jesus and Mary. You are in all my prayers and Masses.

May the blessing of God the Father, Son, and Holy Ghost remain upon you forever.

fr. M. Gerard
Abbot

Archbishop John Gregory Murray of St. Paul invited Abbot Gerard back to his old parish, the Cathedral of St. Paul, to preach on St. Patrick's Day, 1954. In his sermon Father told his listeners that "St. Patrick is celebrated not so much because he was a preacher, a teacher, and the Apostle of Ireland, but because he was a saint — one who lives so as to merit to die in the friendship and good pleasure of God. You should be happy to be alive during this Marian Year. . . . The Fathers of the Church teach that it is the will of God that we receive all things through Mary."

Though he was returning to St. Paul the first time since 1925, he planned to see only his immediate family there. But when his friends found out he was returning, they gathered at centers to see him. They brought him to his former schools, and to St. Paul's Priory, where he visited with Sister Elaine, O.S.B., one of his earliest teachers, and with the other Sisters there. In the letter written after his return to the monastery, Father Gerard told the family what the trip had meant to him.

April 17, 1954

My dear Sisters and Brothers:

I am writing this on Holy Saturday. The Easter zephyrs are already beginning to blow in upon us, and I want to wish you all a very happy Easter — one that will be heart-soothing in time and bloom and blossom into a happy Easter in heaven. Our Holy Week was a beautiful one, as usual. We carry out the liturgy right to the letter, and everything went very smoothly and splendidly this year. It was the first time we had pontifical ceremonies; in fact, it's the first time I've seen pontifical ceremonies for everything.

Syl and Madeline assist at everything, but I did not succeed in getting them over for the tenebrae at two o'clock in the morning. I almost had them over one day, but they both worked so hard that it was impossible for them even to set the alarm at that hour.

Syl was the usher on Good Friday. I saw him, after the adoration of the cross, send the people down the wrong direction, thus sending them home before the Mass of the Presanctified. He told me that some of them were getting rather tired anyway. It was a two-hour service, so they thanked him for sending them down the opposite direction.

I am still living in the memory of our St. Paul visit. It was indeed a beautiful day, one of the outstanding days of my life.

You don't know what a feeling of pleasant memories came over me when I stepped out into the St. Paul depot, where I used to run a soda fountain. Then to go by the Sherman Hotel and down Fourth Street by the library and the armory to the cathedral — all the thoughts and memories of my youth came back to me when passing those streets where I used to walk so frequently.

The Archbishop and Father George Ryan were most kind and most hospitable and thoughtful in every way. God bless them.

It was a very great solace to meet all my seminary companions and professors* before the Mass. . . . I shook their hands in the sacristy while they were vesting for the Mass. Then to be surrounded at the Mass by all my seminary companions was a great joy to me. The deacon was the rector of the seminary; the subdeacon, who is the rector of St. Thomas College, was my golf-playing companion in the early days. The assistant deacons were also seminary companions of mine. Then Monsignor Cullinan (we used to call him "little Johnny" Cullinan) was sitting there in his monsignor's robes. It was surprising to meet them. Some who used to have very wavy hair are now bald, and others now have thin, grey hair. Most of them put on a little weight, also. . . .

I enjoyed the breakfast, too, and particularly the family spirit in which it was given. Above all, I enjoyed the family repast at Mary's in the evening. I am sorry that I was so bothered with those phone calls. It took most of the joy out of the evening. I want to thank Mary, Elaine, and Joan, my good nieces, for all their kindness and hospitality and devotedness during that splendid dinner.

Ag and Ed and I arrived at the seminary just in time to have a little talk with the boys before bedtime. I think I kept them overtime. It was a splendid little visit, and I enjoyed it very much — both with the boys and with the professors. Some newspaper men were there; they listened in and took a picture afterward. I noticed that neither the picture nor their words turned out very well. They got a couple of wrong ideas into the paper. The next morning I said Mass at Nazareth, and I gave Holy

* From Nazareth Hall, St. Paul.

Communion. Then the rector took me to Cretin where I used to go to school. Here I spoke to about eight hundred boys. Then I went to St. Thomas College, around downtown, the Emporium, and the meat market where I used to work on Saturdays. Then we went to the hospital to see a priest who was ill there, a seminary companion of mine, also. Then, finally, Ed and Bart took me to the airport. [In Chicago] . . . I picked up Doctor Law, who came to Our Lady of the Genesee with me and made a little retreat there. I also called Sister Noreen while I was in Chicago. She, Helen, and Madonna were very kind and thoughtful while I was there. . . .

I hope that your Easter joys will be full and that they will never wane, and that everything goes well with you, as well as with us here at Piffard.

We are selling more bread than usual, and Syl just loves to get new customers and to see that they are supplied. He's even got Madeline interested in the project now.

I will be going to Wrentham, Massachusetts, on the tenth of May in order to make the visitation of the Cistercian nuns there. . . .

I think I will drive to Wrentham, as the abbot of Utah will probably meet me there and come home with me to stay a few days.

I am not sure if I will be going to Europe this year or not. I must go next year so I may skip this year, but my plans have not matured yet. If I don't go to Europe, I shall go to Utah on a little visit along in October, *Deo volente*.

The thought that struck me most forcefully during these holy days was the love that Jesus has for our souls. St. Augustine says that if He did not love sinners, He would not have come down from Heaven; and so every time I see the picture of the crib, or a host, or a cross, it ought to remind me of the great love that Jesus has for my soul. He loved me so much as to empty Himself and take the form of a creature in the crib, and He loves me so much as to give Himself to me in His abiding presence in the Holy Eucharist — in the Host — and above all, He loved me when He bowed His head and died upon the cross for my salvation.

We ought to act like a good old brother at Gethsemani. Whenever he'd see a crucifix, he'd stop short, and he'd look at it for some time; then he would make a bow and go on. He was so impressed by the love of Jesus on the cross for His poor creature that he had to pause and thank Him for it and admire His love before he could go on.

I hope that this thought, that Jesus loves you so intensely, will awaken a great return of love in your soul; and remember that love is expressed by doing the will of the beloved. And so I hope that you will be so disposed that you will do all that Jesus asks of you and accept all from His hand of love. This will be a perfect return of His love and will join your soul in a perfect union with His Sacred Heart. I hope that this will be the blessing He will bestow upon you this Eastertide and that your soul will ever rest in peace and joy in doing His will and thus you will all be saints someday in heaven.

Every best blessing upon you.

In the Sacred Hearts
of our Risen Saviour
and our Easter Queen.
fr. M. Gerard,
Abbot

Abbot Gerard acted as visitator for two monasteries in the West in 1954, instead of going to Europe to the general chapter of the Order. On his way to Utah, he stopped at a few of the places where he had spent his early childhood. In a letter to the family on his return to the monastery, he wrote:

I cannot but recall the words of our Lord: "And every one that hath left house, or brethren, or sisters, or father, or mother . . . or lands, for My name's sake, shall receive an hundredfold and shall possess life everlasting." I had offered to our Lord and our Lady all hope in this life of ever returning to those places and persons that had become very dear to me because of close association and early memory. . . . It is only one Trappist out of two hundred who has the opportunity to see again the places that he left before entering the monastery.

I'm sure that if I had remained in the world, I would never have had the keen joys that were mine in revisiting those places, nor would I have received such a hearty welcome from my near and dear ones.

When I was in St. Paul last spring, I felt that I would never have quite so heart-soothing an experience again as that hearty welcome back to St. Paul, to the seminary, and to the cathedral, which I then experienced and enjoyed. It was indeed a small foretaste of the joys of family union in Paradise. I did not realize then that the Marian Year held an even greater happiness for me, which came to me in this visit which I made to the old home places and to Utah. I knew that I would see extraordinary things and experience wonderful happenings during this great year which our dearest Mother has laved over with her goodness and love and maternal solicitude, but I hardly thought that she would arrange something in such a material way as she did. She is ever the lovely Queen — always thinking thoughts of sweetness and goodness towards her children. We will never be able to love her enough in time nor praise her enough in eternity.

She, in her Immaculate Heart, has embodied all the goodness and love and paternity of God Himself, and she has given it a maternal touch.

The end of my sacrifice and prayer and the intention in my Mass during the whole of my life will be that we will all be united in one great family union in heaven, where God will be our Father, Mary our Mother, and the angels and saints our brothers and sisters.

The rest of the letter gave the family a day by day account of his trip. When he returned to the monastery, he wrote, "I am very happy to be back again in old Piffard where I hope to love Jesus and Mary and to honor the Trinity all the rest of my life, and gladly be received in the home of Love where I'll meet you and greet you all some day."

His next trip was to Europe, where he attended the general chapter of the Order. Before leaving he wrote about his plans to the family. It was his last general letter to them.

Our Lady of the Genesee
Piffard, New York
August 27, 1955

My dear Brothers and Sisters,

We are just coming through the octave of the Assumption of our dearest Mother and the octave of the feast of St. Bernard. Both are quite conjoined because of their relation between one another. St. Bernard was Mary's citherist. He sang of her and spoke of her and preached of her as few Fathers of the Church and few other Doctors of the Church. St. Bernard is an outstanding figure in Mariology and an outstanding saint in our Cistercian Order.

The sermon for the feast fell to my lot, and I will summarize it in a few words to you now. I chose as the text, "Mary has chosen the best part." There are two natures, as it were, of man, the divine and the human; or better, two sides to man, the divine and the human. We were never at any time destined for a natural end. Therefore any physical perfection that might be found in us such as eating and growing and propagating the species is not enough to perfect our nature because God has destined us for a supernatural end. Therefore, in orientating our mind and our will to Him, we will find what we are created for— knowledge and love of God.

The upper part of man consists of his soul, his intellect, and his mind; and when they are orientated to God, then man is supernatural, and he will attain his end. Our mind seeks for truth; the end of the mind is truth. The greatest truth that a man can contemplate is the divine, the infinite truth, God. That is why our mind seeks in a natural way to contemplate God.

The end of our will is a good, and the greatest good that a man can apply his soul to is the sovereign good, the greatest good, God. There is in our very nature, says St. Thomas, an initial impulse to love God. We want God because we want that which is good. We want the greatest good; we really want God.

Therefore, if man follows his better self, his real self, he will attain to his supernatural end. He will want to think of God and to love Him. . . .

Sin is a disorientation, a turning away from our proper end. It is an application of our minds to truths aside from God and resting in them as our last end. Therefore, the atheist is really outraging his mind. He is really thwarting it from what he really wants, from what it was created for, the contemplation of truth. The greatest truth we can possibly contemplate is the eternal Truth, Him who contains all truth, who is the norm of every truth because a thing is true . . . inasmuch as it is conformed to the divine mind. So the norm of truth is found in God alone.

When one applies his will to love a creature and only a creature and thinks the creature is his end, then he is thwarting his God-bent will and he is frustrating really the end of his being which is to love good, to love the highest good in a higher manner, to love God supremely, therefore.

It is this best part that Mary chose. She has given us then an example of proper living, of orientating all things to our divine end. Then I went on to show how the contemplative life is the "better part." Someday perhaps I can go over that with you, or perhaps I can send the sermon on to you. But at present I am a little bit short of time because I am on tiptoes to go to New York to board the boat, the *Liberte*, and on to Europe.

I think that if I had been going to Europe fifteen years ago I would have turned somersaults for a year beforehand. But at present I am so occupied that it doesn't bother me too much. It is just like going to another occupation. However, as time approaches, I do get a little concerned about it. The last few days I have been working overtime, straightening up the last things so that I can leave the desk free and cleared before I go.

I will be facing a lot of new things. First of all, the boat ride on the ocean, and the first visit to Europe, and all those places which I have been reading about and hearing about down the years. . . .

I plan now to go first to Paris, to Dijon and to the general chapter. I will take in Lisieux before I go out to the chapter. . . .

Be assured, my dear brothers and sisters, that I will remember you at all the shrines of our Lady and at the holy places when I am over there. Pray that I might come back with more grace and with more wisdom and with good health.

Every good blessing upon you, and be assured that we are

always praying for you here as our good benefactors, having given your brother to the service of the Lord.

In the Sacred Hearts of Jesus and Mary,
fr. M. Gerard, O.C.S.O.
Abbot

IV

LETTERS RELATING TO THE DEATH OF ABBOT GERARD

FROM Notre Dame de Citeaux, France, where the world-wide general chapter for Trappist abbots was in session, Dom James Fox, Abbot of Our Lady of Gethsemani, Trappist, Kentucky, wrote the following letter to the monks of Abbot Gerard's community in Piffard, informing them of the serious illness of their Reverend Father.

September 16, 1955.
Citeaux, France.
Notre Dame de Citeaux.

Dear Fr. Prior:

I must write to you and to your dear community about your good Reverend Father.

You all know better than I that he has been working terrifically all year. He has had pains in his left chest and arm — difficulty in breathing at times. The doctor said his heart was all right, and so your Reverend Father felt more at ease. You know how he "whirl-winded" through his work to clean up all for the general chapter.

When he arrived at Citeaux, I noticed he was quite pale, but he attributed it to the change of food and drink, extra excitement, etc. But he told me that he had not slept for several nights, had difficulty in breathing, no appetite. In fact, he said that he thought he was going to die the night before in Paris. Terrific pains in chest—angina pectoris.

Monday he did not come to the opening Mass of the general chapter. Some one called me out of church and told me that he had fainted. He was carried to his room and wanted to see me.

He was then feeling much better and tried to follow the sessions. However, Wednesday he had to go to bed, and then we realized that it was no passing fatigue, excitement, or indigestion. The doctor came and thought at first it was heart trouble. But later, with Dom Gerard's explanation to help, it seems that it was diabetes, which gradually affects the arteries and impedes their perfect functioning, i.e., the distribution of the blood. This in the chest causes terrific pains and suffocation.

Your good Reverend Father began to get worse and really thought he was going to die. With Dom Robert and myself present, the Most Reverend Abbot General administered extreme unction.

Of course the doctor kept coming from Dijon. The Citeaux infirmarian put a mattress on the floor and slept there each night. One could die in this place and no one would ever know.

Friday we took him to the hospital in Dijon. The doctors are very much concerned about his state. The diabetes complicates everything.

I need not ask you to pray for him. Please have the priest make an *imperatum pro infirmo* and the non-priests include good Reverend Father's condition in their Holy Communion and prayers.

May Jesus and Mary watch over us. Nothing, nothing happens that Jesus does not will or permit and for our best eternal interests.

All for Jesus through Mary, and always with a trustful smile,

fr. James [Abbot of Gethsemani
Trappist, Kentucky]

At noon, September 19, 1955, the following cable announced the death of Abbot Gerard:

YOUR REVEREND FATHER DIED
MONDAY MORNING ABOUT FOUR THIRTY.

The abbot general of the Trappist Cistercians, Reverend Father M. Gabriel, wrote a detailed explanation of the circumstances surrounding the death of the young abbot.

Citeaux, France
Sept. 20, 1955

Dear Father Prior of the Genesee,

I address this letter to you and to the whole community, to all Dom Gerard's sons who mourn his passing, and who long to know the details of their beloved Father's death. At the port, a car from Melleray Abbey awaited Dom Robert and Dom Gerard. Then Dom Robert, tired from the long journey, went by train to Paris, but Dom Gerard to Lisieux. This pilgrimage was so great a joy to Dom Gerard that the father who accompanied him said it was difficult to get him to leave when he was praying at the various shrines where St. Thérèse's relics were venerated. Leaving Lisieux, Dom Gerard said: "Now I can die." Perhaps God gave him a presentiment of his approaching death.

In Paris, Dom Gerard and his companion met Dom Robert. They visited some of the famous churches: Notre Dame Cathedral, Sainte Chapelle, etc. Your Reverend Father remained a long time in Rue du Bac Chapel, where the apparition of our Lady with the miraculous medal occurred. You have heard of it. They arrived here at Citeaux on Sunday evening. I saw Dom Gerard, and he seemed well. He appeared to be in good health and looked better than when I had seen him at Gethsemani or Genesee.

As we went to church for the Mass of the Holy Spirit on Monday morning, he felt a great weariness and went to rest. However, he felt well enough to attend the sessions. That evening he showed me the architect's first plan for the permanent buildings of your monastery. The weariness that he felt in the morning passed. Monday night was difficult — he slept badly. I excused him from the remaining sessions. On Wednesday he remained in bed, but he was very eager to take part in the voting. For this reason I gave him my room near the council room, and took his own. The doctor came twice a day. He was very anxious. Dom Gerard's heart seemed to be in poor condition, and with the complications of diabetes the case was serious.

Your Reverend Father asked me to administer extreme unction. On Wednesday evening, just before Compline, he received the Sacrament. There were only the abbots of Gethesmani, Holy Ghost, and Melleray with us. He wished to receive *in privatim*. Soon it became necessary to take him to Dijon, to a clinical hospital, but we feared for his heart. Then, on Friday, he seemed better and a car took him to the clinic. The doctors there did all they could, but they told me that they were very much concerned about his condition. At first, Dom James of Gethsemani stayed with him at the clinic. When he had to go to Paris, Dom Robert took his place. I visited Dom Gerard each day. I believe that everything possible was done for him, but the case was desperate. Then came a poison-crisis. The day before yesterday in the morning, he was better, but in the evening the hospital sent me an urgent call: his condition was becoming worse. We spent the night near him, Dom Robert, my secretary and I; two doctors and sisters attended him, but at 4:35 A.M. on Monday, our dear patient went to God. I dressed him myself, and we offered our Masses for him. During his illness he never complained — never said a word about getting well. He trusted completely in God's will. He offered his life for the success of the general chapter, for the Order, for his monastery. I asked him during the last night to accept his death for all his sons, and he said very distinctly that he would do so. They were his last words. Dom Robert whispered invocations to him, and he repeated them very softly. Then in a louder voice we heard him say: "Jesus, Mary and Joseph." I shall always remember him and his most edifying death.

Dear sons, I pray to our Lord for all of you. His will is adorable, both when He comforts us and when He tries us. May Mary our Mother save you. I bless you paternally.

fr. M. Gabriel,
Abbot General, Trappist-Cistercians

Because of the large number of inquiries from people who had come to know and love the late Abbot Gerard, the prior at Our Lady of the Genesee in Piffard, Father M. Regis Tompkins, prepared a letter to send to friends and acquaintances, giving details of the last days of their Reverend Father. Excerpts of the letter are given here.

JESUS

DOM M. GERARD MC GINLEY, O.C.S.O.

Our Lady of the Genesee Abbey
Piffard, New York

Dear friends:

Following the sudden death of our beloved Abbot, Dom Gerard McGinley, many of you sent words of sympathy and expressed the desire to receive a more complete account of his illness and death. We of Our Lady of the Genesee are glad to fulfill your desire; this letter will tell you something of the last days of a man who inspired so many souls to a generous love of God by his own simplicity, self-sacrificing charity, and humility.

Dom Gerard, with all the enthusiasm of youth, began to prepare for his first general chapter. There was much to be done before he was to say good-bye to his sons. Correspondence had piled high (it was only once or twice a year that he was able to see the top of his desk). Then, too, he was busy with packing and caring for the many details of the building program (a new barn and a new bakery) which was in full sway. Yes, Dom Gerard was a very busy man during those last few weeks, but his children never failed to see him with his gentle smile. He radiated his excitement to his sons and often talked of the shrines he would visit and the little talk that he planned to have with the Holy Father. In a letter he remarked that this was to be a trip of many firsts, "my first trip across the ocean; first trip to France; my first trip to Lisieux; my first trip to Rome." And the saints in heaven were adding, "his first trip to Paradise."

Finally the day arrived and Dom Gerard breathed a sigh of relief. The desk was cleaned and all was packed. He had even learned to operate all the gadgets on the camera which he was going to use to bring back the scenes from his trip to his sons he was leaving behind. On August 31 in the late morning he hurriedly gave his blessing to several monks who had gathered at the office for his departure. With suitcase in hand, he walked out briskly into the light summer rain, turned and waved his last blessing upon the monks who were peering through the windows of the abbey cloister; and passing the statue of the Sacred Heart in the garden he disappeared through the gate house door.

When Dom Gerard boarded the *Liberte,* a French liner, just before noon on September third, he was not a well man. He had remarked to a nun at the monastery of the Precious Blood where he celebrated the community Mass on the morning of the first that he had been airsick on the plane to New York. Then, too, earlier in the month of August he was troubled by a hemorrhage in the retina of his left eye and had entered the hospital for a few days "just for a check up." Several times preceding his departure he interrupted his Mass to allow a feeling of nausea to pass. But as he always minimized his own sufferings, even those close to him did not realize that this condition might be serious.

During the passage across the Atlantic Dom Gerard experienced several bad nights with pains in his chest and difficulty in his breathing. Dom Robert McGann, his traveling companion, noticed that he was not able to recite his breviary because of the condition of his eyes. Previously he had asked his monks to pray for his eyes as his front vision was obscure. He was planning to bathe in the waters of Our Lady of Lourdes, confident that she would hear his prayers.

The days of the sea voyage had passed and the *Liberte* was soon to land. The passengers were busy getting their suitcases and trunks prepared for customs. In the excitement that always accompanies a landing and debarkation of an ocean liner, Dom Gerard stole a few precious moments to write a short note in his usual carefree style to his children back home in the Genesee Valley. "Somewhere on the French or British coast — we will land in five hours. (I'm going to our 'stateroom,' alias cabin, to finish this; it is shaking up here terribly. I'm in the salon — I'm not shaking; I insist it is the boat.) I get French lessons in the salon every day from the president of the French Boy Scouts. A French salon is not an American saloon, mind you! We are landing! ! ! All is excitement! In France! Debarking! Calling! Going! Love to all, and blessings. Father Mary Gerard."

They arrived at the Abbey of Citeaux a short distance from Paris on Sunday, September 11. In this age-old abbey all the Cistercian abbots were gathering for their annual general chapter, the supreme authority in the Cistercian Order. This year was to be a plenary chapter, that is, a chapter at which all should attend unless they were excused by the most pressing business.

Dom James, the Father Immediate of Our Lady of the Genesee, met Reverend Father shortly after his arrival at Citeaux. He thought that Dom Gerard looked rather pale, but attributed it to the excitement of the trip and the change of food. Reverend Father told him of the difficult nights he had experienced on the boat and how he had thought that he was going to die during the night in Paris. But because Dom Gerard was never one to complain, Dom James thought it was just a remark in passing, and did not take him seriously.

Monday morning, September 12, the first day of the general chapter, the abbots were singing the votive Mass of the Holy Spirit to implore light on the very important tasks they were about to begin, when Dom James was called out of church and was told that Dom Gerard had fainted. Our Reverend Father had been taken to his room, and had regained consciousness, and had asked for Dom James. When Dom James arrived at his room he found our Reverend Father smiling and feeling much better. In fact he felt so well that by evening he was absorbed in the pleasant task of showing the first plans of the permanent monastery of Our Lady of the Genesee to the Most Reverend Abbot General. He explained how the architect that had prepared the plans was to join him after the general chapter and that they would make a tour of the ancient abbeys in France to get some ideas to use in the new monastery.

That night Dom Gerard again experienced those severe pains in the chest which made breathing so difficult and in the morning his strength was almost exhausted. But this was his first general chapter, and he was determined that he would not spend it in bed. He attended some of the sessions that day but continued to get worse. Reverend Father General dispensed him from attending the remaining meetings, but insisted that Dom Gerard change rooms with himself so that Dom Gerard could be nearer the council room to take part more easily in the voting.

On the morning of the fourteenth he said his last Mass. Shortly after, he was confined to bed. The Doctor was called from nearby Dijon and did not conceal the fact that he was very worried about Reverend Father's condition. Dom Gerard knew that he was seriously ill and asked the Abbot General to administer extreme unction. Just before Compline that evening he received the sacrament from Reverend Father General with Dom James, Dom Robert, and Dom Louis Gonzaga, Abbot of Melleray, present.

Owing to the gravity of his condition he was moved to the clinical hospital in Dijon so that he could be watched constantly by the trained staff. . . .

Dom Robert McGann, who had been Reverend Father's novice master at Gethsemani years before, relieved Dom James at the sick bed on Saturday and when Dom James returned Sunday morning, the patient was cheerful and seemed much better. He still had no appetite and the Sisters could not get him to take food. . . .

At Citeaux Sunday evening about 8 o'clock, Reverend Father General received an urgent phone call from the hospital; Dom Gerard's condition was becoming worse. The doctor said that he had no chance to recover but a certain potent injection that he wanted to administer might prolong his life four or five days. He did not want to give it without the permission of the Abbot General.

Reverend Father General went at once to the hospital and after a short consultation he gave the necessary permission. The injection brought immediate relief from the chest pains but the doctor shortly after remarked that he doubted that he would be alive by 5 o'clock the next morning. . . .

The first rays of dawn were appearing in the sky to the east of the little village of Dijon when at 4:35 on the morning of the nineteenth of September Dom Gerard quietly passed from his earthly exile into the arms of God.

When the monks of Our Lady of the Genesee in the early

morning of September nineteenth chanted the solemn Office of the Dead to mark the beginning of the "Solemn Tricenary" — a month of prayers for the deceased members of the Order, for relatives and benefactors, who had died during the year — little did they realize that they were singing the Office for their Father Abbot who had died in a hospital in far away France some few hours before.

It was shortly before dinner on September nineteenth that Father Prior received the cryptic cablegram from Father General. The cable read, "Your Reverend Father died Monday morning about four-thirty. Signed Abbot General." Father Prior, unable to believe the message, asked the clerk at Western Union to repeat the message and to check through to see if it were actually true before he would make the sad announcement to the community. When there was no doubt that it was true, the community was assembled for an extraordinary chapter by the ringing of the great bell of the church. Only God can know the suffering he asked of the sons of our dear Reverend Father on that day and the days that followed; for Dom Gerard was a true Father to all his sons and had won the hearts of all of us. Though our hearts were crushed we knew that he had attained that for which he had striven so beautifully through the thirty years of his religious life, that beatitude and unending peace for which we are all striving. . . .

The body of our Reverend Father arrived in New York harbor on October third, the feast of the Little Flower. A delegation of laymen from Rochester and vicinity, led by Father Joseph Cirrincione, close friends of Reverend Father and our community, went down to New York to meet the boat, to receive the body and to act as escort to Rochester. It was early evening on October fourth when the remains of our Reverend Father arrived at the abbey gates.

The community with Dom James as celebrant went out to meet the body. After the blessings and prayers, the procession moved back to the church, the casket was placed near the presbytery step; and just as the community began to chant the Office of Compline, the casket was opened, and his sons looked once again upon the face of their beloved Father. After the *Salve* the casket was moved to the communion rail of the secular chapel so that the many visitors could view the remains; two monks began the night watch and the recitation of the Psalms for the repose of his soul. With the body again in the choir the following day, Dom James sang a pontifical Requiem Mass for Reverend Father. This was followed by the absolution of the deceased according to the Cistercian rite. In the afternoon the body, accompanied by Father Prior, by Reverend Father's immediate family, and some close friends, was moved to the cathedral in Rochester. When the funeral cortege reached the cathedral at 4 o'clock, the bell was tolling, the Fourth Degree Knights of Columbus were lined up to act as pall bearers, and Bishop Kearney was waiting at the church in mitre and cope to meet the corpse, to give the blessing, and to recite the prayers for such a reception.

That evening the priests of the Rochester diocese gathered in the cathedral to recite the Office of the Dead for the man they had grown to love and revere in the four years since the foundation of Our Lady of the Genesee.

It was raining heavily on the morning of the sixth when the monks of Our Lady of the Genesee boarded the buses which were to carry them to Rochester for the pontifical Requiem Mass to be celebrated by Bishop Kearney. Despite the rain, a large crowd gathered in the cathedral for the funeral Mass. It was just a little less than two years since many of them had come to attend his abbatial blessing and the contrast between the two occasions was striking.

After the Mass, Bishop Kearney preached a beautiful eulogy on Reverend Father, taking for his text, "Unless you become as little children, you cannot enter into the kingdom of heaven." He remarked that the diocese of Rochester owes the first abbot of Our Lady of the Genesee a great debt of gratitude for establishing the Trappist life among them and for the numerous times he sacrificed his time to speak at religious gatherings and explain our life to those who did not understand it.

Just before the procession came out of the church the rain ceased and did not begin again until an hour or so after the burial. For this favor the monks were very grateful to God, for it was then possible to hold the ceremonies at the grave.

About thirty-five or forty cars followed the hearse and the two buses carrying the religious back to the monastery, a trip of thirty miles. A large group of people had already assembled when they arrived.

Bishop Lawrence Casey, Auxiliary Bishop of Rochester, conducted the ceremonies at the grave according to the Cistercian rite. The hearse followed the two rows of monks as they made their way slowly to the little cemetery, as they went in procession. Although women could not enter the cemetery since it is within the enclosure, a place was provided for them alongside the enclosure fence from which they could view the burial.

It was about 1:30 on the afternoon of October sixth when the body of our beloved Reverend Father was laid to rest beside the saintly religious that had gone before him, Father Simon and Frater Dennis. Now the third white cross looks out over the Genesee Valley which Dom Gerard loved to call the Valley of Mary's Smile.

Let us not forget him in death whom we loved in life.

Sincerely in Jesus and Mary,
The Community
Our Lady of the Genesee Abbey
Piffard, New York